THE CALL OF THE BEAVER PATROL

Or, A Break in the Glacier

CAPT. V. T. SHERMAN

1st WORLD
LIBRARY
Literary Society

The Call of the Beaver Patrol

V. T. Sherman

© 1st World Library, 2008
PO Box 2211
Fairfield, IA 52556
www.1stworldlibrary.com
First Edition

LCCN: 2007935411

Softcover ISBN: 978-1-4218-9365-5
Hardcover ISBN: 978-1-4218-9465-2
eBook ISBN: 978-1-4218-9265-8

Purchase *"The Call of the Beaver Patrol"*
as a traditional bound book at:
www.1stWorldLibrary.com/purchase.asp?ISBN=978-1-4218-9365-5

1st World Library is a literary, educational organization
dedicated to:

- Creating a free internet library of downloadable ebooks

- Hosting writing competitions and offering book publishing
scholarships.

Interested in more 1st World Library books? contact:
literacy@1stworldlibrary.com
Check us out at: www.1stworldlibrary.com

1ˢᵗ World Library Literary Society

Giving Back to the World

"If you want to work on the core problem, it's early school literacy."

- James Barksdale, former CEO of Netscape

"No skill is more crucial to the future of a child, or to a democratic and prosperous society, than literacy."

- Los Angeles Times

"Literacy... means far more than learning how to read and write... The aim is to transmit... knowledge and promote social participation."

- UNESCO

"Literacy is not a luxury, it is a right and a responsibility. If our world is to meet the challenges of the twenty-first century we must harness the energy and creativity of all our citizens."

- President Bill Clinton

"Parents should be encouraged to read to their children, and teachers should be equipped with all available techniques for teaching literacy, so the varying needs and capacities of individual kids can be taken into account."

- Hugh Mackay

CONTENTS

CHAPTER I

CAMPING IN THE BREAKER

"And so I says to myself, says I, give me a good husky band of Boy Scouts! They'll do the job if it can be done!"

Case Canfield, caretaker, sat back in a patched chair in the dusky, unoccupied office of the Labyrinth mine and addressed himself to four lads of seventeen who were clad in the khaki uniform of the Boy Scouts of America.

Those of our readers who have read the previous books of this series will have good cause to remember George Benton, Charley ("Sandy") Green, Tommy Gregory and Will Smith. The adventures of these lads among the Pictured Rocks of Old Superior, among the wreckers and reptiles of the Florida Everglades, in the caverns of the Great Continental Divide, and among the snows of the Hudson Bay wilderness have been recorded under appropriate titles in previous works.

The four boys were members of the Beaver Patrol, Chicago. Will Smith was Scoutmaster, while George Benton was Patrol Leader. They wore upon the sleeves of their coats medals showing that they had passed the examination as Ambulance Aids, Stalkers, Pioneers and Seamen.

Instructed by Mr. Horton, a well-known criminal lawyer of Chicago, the boys had reached the almost deserted mine at dusk of a November day. There they had found Canfield, the caretaker, waiting for them in a dimly-lighted office. The mine had not been operated for a number of months, not because the veins had given out, but because of some misunderstanding between the owners of mines in that section.

The large, bare room in which the caretaker and the Boy Scouts met was in the breaker. There was no fire in the great heater, and the tables and chairs were black with dust. A single electric light shone down from the ceiling, creating long, ghostlike shadows as it swayed about in a gentle wind blowing through a broken window.

"Well," Tommy Gregory said, as the caretaker paused, "you've got the Boy Scouts, and it remains for you to set us to work."

"And a sturdy looking lot, too!" grinned the caretaker.

"Oh, Mr. Horton wouldn't be apt to send a lot of cripples!" laughed Sandy Green. "He's next to his job, that man is!"

"I presume he told you all about the case?" suggested Canfield.

"Indeed he did not," replied Will Smith.

"Not a thing about it?" asked the caretaker.

"He only said that you would give us full instructions."

"That's strange!" Canfield observed thoughtfully.

"Perhaps he thought we wouldn't want to undertake the job if we knew exactly what it was!" suggested Sandy.

"It is a queer kind of a job," Canfield admitted, "but I don't think you boys would be apt to back out because of a little danger."

"I have wanted to back out several times," laughed Tommy, "but, somehow, these others boys wouldn't permit me to."

"Go on and tell us about it," urged Sandy. "Tell us just what you want us to do, and then we'll tell you whether we think we can do it or not."

"You've got to find two boys!" replied Canfield.

"Mother of Moses!" exclaimed Tommy. "I hope we haven't got to go and dig up blond-haired little Algernon, or discover pretty little Clarence, and turn a bunch of money over to him!"

"I think these two boys may have money coming to them," the caretaker replied. "There must be money back of it or the friends of the lads wouldn't be giving me cash to spend in their interest."

"Where are these boys?" asked Will.

"I've heard the opinion expressed that the boys are somewhere in the mine!" answered Canfield. "I can hardly believe that they are, but it has been suggested that we may as well begin the search under ground."

"Where do these boys belong?" asked George.

"Anywhere and everywhere," was the reply. "Jimmie Maynard

and Dick Thompson came here as breaker boys six months ago. They were ragged and dirty, and appeared to be as tough as two young bears. They worked steadily until the day before the mine closed down and then they disappeared."

"That's easy!" declared Tommy. "They got tired of work!"

"That may be," answered the caretaker, "but they certainly didn't get tired of drawing their pay. They went away leaving about eight dollars, the two of them, in the care of the company."

"Then something must have happened to them!" Will suggested.

"Who's looking for these boys?" asked George.

"A New York lawyer," was the reply. "I know nothing whatever about the man. In fact, I don't know why he wants to find out where the boys are. He sends me money and tells me to continue my quest until the boys are found, and then to send them to New York."

"So you have entire charge of the search," said Sandy, tentatively.

"Yes," was the reply, "except for Joe Ventner. He's a detective sent on from New York by this Burlingame person, the lawyer to whom I referred a short time ago."

"What part of the world is he searching?" asked Will.

"He seems to think that the boys ran away because of some childish prank put on by them the night before. They broke some windows in a couple of shanties down by the tracks, or, at least, the other boys say they did, and Joe thinks they ran

V. T. Sherman

away because of that. He accounts in that way for their not calling after their pay envelopes."

"So he thinks they've gone out of the country, does he."

"Yes," was the reply. "He comes back here every few days to ask if I have heard anything regarding the youngsters, and then goes away again. If you leave it to me, I don't think the fellow is working very hard in the case. There's a half a dozen saloons in a little dump of a place about ten miles away, and my idea is that he puts in a good deal of his time there."

"You don't seem to take to this detective?" asked George.

"Oh, I don't know as he's so much worse than the average private detective," replied the caretaker. "He's out for his day's wages, and the easier he can get them, the better it suits him.

"So you don't know who wants these boys, or what they're wanted for?" asked Will. "Lawyer Burlingame never took you into his confidence so far as to post you on the details of the case."

"He never did!" answered the caretaker.

"Is he liberal with his money?" asked George.

"He pays all the bills I send in," was the answer. "And seems to keep this bum detective pretty well supplied with ten-dollar bills."

"We may have to investigate this investigator!" laughed Sandy.

"Did Mr. Horton say anything to you about your lodgings while here?" asked the caretaker. "It's getting too cold here for me, and we may as well be shifting to warmer quarters."

"You said a short time ago," Will began, "that you rather thought we ought to begin this search in the mine itself."

"That's my idea!" answered the caretaker.

"Do you think the boys are hiding in the mine?"

"Well, there are some things connected with the case which point in that direction," replied Canfield. "For instance, there's a lot of queer things going on under ground."

"Ghosts?" demanded Tommy.

"You're not steering us up against a haunted mine, are you?" asked George with a wink at his chum. "That would be too good to be true!"

"I haven't said anything about ghosts or haunted mines," chuckled the caretaker. "I'm only saying that there are queer things taking place in the mine. Now there's Tunnel Six," he went on, "I have seen lights there with my own eyes, when I know there wasn't a person within two miles of the spot except myself. And I've heard noises, too! These unaccountable noises which make a man think of graveyards and ghosts."

"But why should two healthy, active boys want to seek such a hiding place?" asked Will. "It certainly can't be very pleasant in the dark and damp tunnels! Besides, where would they get their provisions?"

"I'm not arguing the case, lads," the caretaker replied, "I'm placing the case in your hands without instructions. I only suggest that you look in the mine first, but you don't have to do that unless you want to!"

"I don't see how we can find fault with that arrangement!" laughed Will. "And now," he went on, "let's arrange about our lodgings. In the first place, who knows that we are here on this job?"

"Not a soul, unless some one saw you coming into the breaker!"

"That's just as it should be," Will went on. "Now I propose that we camp out in the breaker. There must be a cosy corner somewhere, under the chutes, or in back of a staircase, or away up under the roof, where we can camp out while we are going through the mine."

"You won't find the old breaker a very comfortable place to live in," suggested Canfield.

"Oh, we can line the walls of some little cubby-hole with canvas if necessary, and you can string a wire in so as to give us electricity for heating and lighting, and we can live as comfortable as four bugs in a rug. If we keep out of sight during the day time, no one will ever suspect that we are here."

"Have it your own way!" replied Canfield. "I'll see that you get plenty to eat and plenty of bed clothing."

"That'll help some!" laughed Tommy. "During the night we can travel through the mine with our lights, and during the daytime we can crawl into our little beds and sleep our heads off!"

"When do you want your first load of provisions?" asked Canfield.

"Right now, tonight!" replied Sandy.

"Well, come along then," Canfield said, rising from his chair, "and I'll let you pick out a spot for your camp, as you call it."

After quite an extended search through the breaker the boys selected a small room on the ground floor, from which one window looked out on the half-deserted yard where the weigh-house stood. The room was perhaps twenty feet in size each way, and the walls were of heavy planking. The whole apartment was sadly in need of a scrubbing, but the lads concluded to postpone that until some future date.

"I can bring in cot beds and bedding," the caretaker announced, "and string the electric wire for heating, lighting, and cooking before I go to bed. That will leave you all shipshape in the morning, and you can then begin your cleaning up as soon as you please."

The caretaker was as good as his word, and before ten o'clock the cots and bedding were in place, also an electric heater and an electric plate for cooking had been moved into the apartment.

Not considering it advisable to go out for supper, Canfield had also brought in provisions in the shape of bacon, potatoes, eggs, bread, butter, coffee, and various grades of canned goods, so the boys had made a hearty meal and had plenty left for breakfast. While cooking they had covered the one window with a heavy piece of canvas.

"Now you're all tight and snug for the night," the caretaker smiled, as he turned back from the door and glanced over the

V. T. Sherman

rather cozy-looking room. "If I'm about here during the night, I'll look in upon you again."

Canfield stepped out and closed the door behind him. Then he came back and looked in again with a half-smile on his face.

"Do you boys know anything about mines?" he asked.

"Not a thing!" replied Tommy.

"Then don't you go climbing down the ladders and wandering around in the gangways tonight!" the caretaker warned.

"Say, there's an idea!" Tommy said to Sandy, with a wink, as Canfield went out. "How do you think one of these mammoth coal mines looks, anyway?"

"Cut that out, boys!" exclaimed Will. "If I catch one of you attempting the ladders tonight, I'll tie you up!"

"Who said anything about going down the ladders tonight?" demanded Tommy.

CHAPTER II

THE CALL OF THE PACK

It was somewhere near midnight when the boys sought their beds. Will and George were soon asleep, but Tommy and Sandy had no notion of passing their first night in the mine in slumber. Ten minutes after the regular breathing of the two sleepers became audible, Tommy sat up in his bed and deftly threw a pillow so as to strike Sandy in the face.

"Cut it out!" whispered Sandy. "You don't have to do anything to wake me up! I've been wondering for a long time whether you hadn't gone to sleep! You looked sleepy when the light went out."

"Never was so wide awake in my life!" declared Tommy.

"Well, get up and dress," advised Sandy. "If we get into the mine tonight, we'll have to hurry!"

"Have you figured out how we're going to get into the mine?" asked Tommy. "It will be the ladders for us, I guess."

"Of course it'll be the ladders!" replied Sandy. "Do you suppose Canfield is coming here in the middle of the night to turn on the power?"

V. T. Sherman

"I wonder how deep the shaft is?" asked Tommy.

"I guess this one must be about five hundred feet."

"Is that a guess, or a piece of positive information?"

"It's a guess," laughed Sandy, drawing on his shoes and walking softly across the bare floor in the direction of the shaft.

The boys passed out of the sleeping chamber into a passage which led directly to the shaft of the mine. This shaft was perhaps twenty feet in width. It included the air shaft, the division where the pumps were operated, and two divisions for the cages which lifted the coal from the bottom of the mine. The pumps were not working, of course, and no air was being forced down.

One of the cages lay at the top so the other must have been at the bottom of the shaft. As the boys looked down into the shaft, Tommy seized his chum by the arm and whispered:

"Did you see that light down there?"

"Light nothing!" declared Sandy.

"But I did see a light!" insisted the other.

"Perhaps you did," replied Sandy, "but if there's any light there it's merely a reflection from our electrics. There may be a metallic surface down there which throws back the light rays."

"Have it your own way!" grunted Tommy. "You know yourself that the caretaker said there were lights in the mine which no one could account for, and he especially mentioned the light in Tunnel Six."

"All right!" Sandy grinned. "We'll sneak down so quietly that any person who happens to be at the bottom of the shaft with the light will never suspect that we are within a hundred miles of the place. We may be able to geezle the fellow that's making the ghost walk around here nights."

The boys took to the ladders and moved down as silently as possible. Now and then a rung creaked softly under their feet, but they got to the bottom without any special mishap.

Tommy drew a long breath when at last they landed at the bottom of the shaft. He threw his light upward, then, and declared that in his opinion they were at least ten thousand feet nearer the center of the earth than they were when they started down.

"I remember now," Sandy said with a grin, "that the Labyrinth mine is only about five hundred feet deep. If I remember correctly, there are three levels; one at three hundred feet; one at four, and one at five."

"And which level is this?" asked Tommy.

"Why, we're on the bottom, ain't we?"

"Of course," laughed Tommy. "I ought to have known that!"

"Well come along if you want to see the mine!" urged Sandy. "All we have to do is to push our searchlights ahead and walk down the gangway. We'll come to something worth seeing after a while."

As the boys advanced they found the gangway considerably cluttered with "gob," or refuse, and the air was none of the best.

"I wish we could set the air shaft working," suggested Sandy.

"Well, we can't!" Tommy answered with a scornful shrug of his shoulders. "We can't set the whole works going in order to give us a midnight view of the Labyrinth mine. What gets me is, how are we going to find our way back? There seem to be a good many passages here."

"I've got that fixed all right!" Sandy exclaimed.

As the lad spoke he took a ball of strong string from his pocket and tied one end to the cage which lay at the bottom of the shaft.

"Now we can go anywhere we please," he chuckled "and when we want to return, all we've got to do is to follow the string."

"Quite an idea!" laughed Tommy.

The boys proceeded along the gangway, walking between the rails of the tramway by means of which the coal was delivered at the bottom of the shaft. The experience was a novel one to them. The dark walls of the passage, the echoes which came from the counter gangways, the monotonous dripping of water as it seeped through seams and crevices in the rock, all gave a weird and uncanny expression to the place.

After walking for some distance the boys came to a level which showed several inches of water.

"We can't wade through that!" Tommy declared.

"Well," Sandy suggested, "if we go back a little ways, we can follow a cross heading and get into the mine by another way."

The boys followed this plan, and, after winding about several half-loaded cars which had been left on the tramway, found themselves in a large chamber from which numerous benches were cut.

"Where does all this gas come from?" asked Tommy stopping short and putting a hand to his nose.

"There must be a blower somewhere," Sandy explained.

"What's a blower?" demanded Tommy. "What does it look like, and does it always smell like this?"

"It doesn't look like anything!" replied Sandy. "It's composed of natural gas, and they call it a blower because it blows up out of crevices in the coal and in the rocks."

"If I should light a match, would it set it on fire?" asked Tommy.

"I wouldn't like to have you try it!"

The boys continued on their way for some moments, and then Tommy stopped and extinguished his light, whispering to Sandy to do the same.

"What's that for?" demanded the latter.

"Didn't you hear that noise behind the cribbing?" asked Tommy.

"Rats, probably!"

"Rats nothing!" replied Tommy. "Rats don't make sounds like people whispering, do they? Keep still a minute, and we'll find out what it is!"

"You'll be seeing a light next!" Sandy suggested.

"I see it now!" answered Tommy.

Sandy saw it, too, in a moment. It seemed at first to be floating in the air at the very top of the gangway. It moved from side to side, and finally dropped down nearer to the floor. There seemed to be no one near it or under it. Its small circle of illumination showed only the empty air.

"What do you make of it?" asked Tommy.

"Is this Tunnel Six?" asked his chum.

"I don't know! If it is, we've seen the light the caretaker referred to. We'll have a great story to tell in the morning!"

The boys stood in the darkness of the gangway watching the light for what seemed to them to be a long time. Now the light advanced toward them, now it receded. Now it lifted to the roof of the gangway, now it dropped almost to the floor.

At intervals, the noises behind the cribbing to which Tommy had referred were repeated, and the boys at last moved over so as to stand with their ears almost against the wooden walls.

"There is some one behind the cribbing, all right!" Tommy declared. "I hear some one breathing."

"Aw, keep still!" whispered Sandy. "If there is anyone there, you'll frighten them away! I thought I heard some one myself!"

"I'll tell you what I think," Tommy suggested in a moment, "and that is that either Will and George, or both of them, beat us to this gangway. They are hiding behind there on purpose to give us a scare."

"That's a dream!" replied Sandy. "We left them both asleep."

"Dream, is it?" repeated Tommy scornfully. "You just listen to the sound that comes from behind this cribbing, and tell me what you make of it!"

Both boys listened intently for a moment, and then Sandy switched on his light and moved swiftly along the cribbing as if in search of an opening. Tommy gazed at him in astonishment.

"You've gone and done it now!" he said.

"There's some one in here all right!" Sandy explained. "Did you hear the call of the pack a minute ago? There are Boy Scouts in there, and what we hear are the signals of the Wolf Patrol."

"That's right!" cried Tommy excitedly. "That's right!"

V. T. Sherman

CHAPTER III

WHO CUT THE STRING?

"Do you suppose he would understand the call of the Beaver Patrol?" asked Sandy. "I'm going to try him, anyway!"

The boy brought his hands together in imitation of the slap of a beaver's tail on the water, and listened for some reply.

"He'll understand that if he's up on Boy Scout literature," suggested Sandy. "He ought to be wise to the signs of the different patrols if he's a good Boy Scout."

There was a short silence, broken only by the constant drip of the water in an adjoining chamber, and then the call of the pack came again, clearly, sharply and apparently only a short distance away.

"What did Mr. Canfield call those two boys we are looking after?" asked Sandy, after waiting a short time for the repetition of the sound.

"Jimmie Maynard and Dick Thompson," replied Tommy.

Sandy threw out his chest and cried out at the top of his lungs:

"Hello, Jimmie! Hello, Dick!"

The lad's voice echoed dismally throughout the labyrinth of passages, but there was no other reply. Tommy and Sandy gave the call of the Beaver Patrol repeatedly, but the call of the Wolf pack was heard no more.

"I'll bet it's some trick!" exclaimed Sandy after waiting in the chamber for a long time in the hope of hearing another call from the boys who were hidden somewhere behind the cribbing.

"What do you mean by trick?" demanded Tommy.

"Why, I mean that some of the breaker boys, out of work because of the stoppage of operations, may have sneaked into the mine on purpose to produce the impression that there are ghosts here."

"But ghosts wouldn't be giving signals of the Wolf Pack, would they?" asked Tommy.

"Not unless they were Scouts," replied the other.

"Oh well, of course the kids would want to test us, wouldn't they, seeing that we were only boys?"

"Well, we've discovered one thing by coming down," said Tommy, "and that is that there really are people in the mine who have no business here."

"Then we may as well go back to bed," advised Sandy.

"Do you know how many corners we've turned since we came in here?" asked Tommy.

"About a thousand, I guess," replied Sandy.

"Yes, and we'd have a fine old time getting out if you hadn't brought that ball of twine!"

"Tell you what we'll do," Sandy said, as the boys turned their faces down the gangway, "we'll pass around the next shoulder of rock and then shut off our lights. Perhaps the kids who gave the cry of the pack in there will then show their light again."

"That's a good idea, too!"

The boys came at length to a brattice, which is a screen, of either wood or heavy cloth, set up in a passage to divert the current of air to a bench where workmen are engaged, and dodged down behind it, first shutting off their lights, of course.

"Now, come on with your old light," whispered Tommy.

As if in answer to the boy's challenge, the light showed again, apparently but a few yards away from their hiding place.

A moment later the call of the pack, sounding louder than before, rang through the passage. The boys sprang to their feet and switched on their lights.

"Why don't you come out and show yourselves?" shouted Tommy.

"I don't believe you're Scouts at all!" declared Sandy.

There was no answer. The boys could hear the drip of water and the purring of the current as it crept into a lower gangway, but that was all.

"That settles it for tonight!" exclaimed Tommy. "I'm not going to hang around here waiting for Boy Scouts who don't respond to signals!"

"That's me!" agreed Sandy. "We'll go to bed and think the matter over. There may be some way of trapping those fellows."

"Suppose it should be Jimmie Maynard and Dick Thompson?" asked Tommy.

"Then we'd have the case closed up in a jiffy!" was the reply.

Before leaving that particular chamber, Tommy selected a large round piece of "gob," placed it in the center of the open space, and laid another small piece of shale on top of it.

"What are you doing that for?" demanded Sandy.

"Don't you know your Indian signs?" demanded the boy. "That means 'This is the trail.' Now I'll put a stone to the right, and that will tell these imitation Boy Scouts to turn to the right if they want to get out."

"I guess they can get out if they want to," suggested Sandy.

Thirty or forty feet further on, where, following the string, the boys turned again, this time to the left, Tommy laid another signal which showed the direction to be taken.

"There," he said with a grin, "we've started them on the right path. If they don't want to follow it, that isn't our fault!"

"We must be getting pretty near the shaft," Sandy said, after

V. T. Sherman

the boys had walked for nearly half an hour on the backward track.

"Pull on your string," suggested Tommy, "and see if it stiffens up like only a short length of it remained out."

Sandy did as requested, and then dropped to the floor with his searchlight laid along the extension of the cord.

"The other end is loose!" he said in a tone of alarm.

"Loose?" echoed Tommy. "How did it ever get loose?"

Sandy sat down on the floor of the passage and began drawing the cord in, hand over hand.

"I'm going to see if it's been cut!" he said.

Tommy stepped on the swiftly moving cord and held it fast to the floor.

"You mustn't draw it in!" he exclaimed. "As long as it lies on the floor as we strung it out, we can follow it without taking any chances. If you pull it in, then it's all off."

"I understand!" Sandy agreed. "I didn't pull much of it in."

The boys started up the gangway, one of them keeping a searchlight on the white thread of cord.

They seemed to make a great many turns and once or twice Sandy declared that they were walking round and round in a circle.

"I don't believe the passages run so we could walk around in a circle!" argued Tommy. "That ain't the way they run passages in mines!"

"I don't care!" Sandy insisted. "We've been turning to the left about all the time, and if you leave it to me, we'll presently come out in the chamber where we heard the call of the pack!"

"That may be right," admitted Tommy. "It does seem as if we'd been turning to the left most of the time. Besides," he went on, "we've been walking long enough to have reached the shaft three or four times."

"And yet," argued Sandy, "we've been following the line of the cord every step. It lies right in the middle of the gangway here, and we're going the way it points all the time."

This bit of reasoning seemed to give the boys fresh courage, and they walked on, expecting every moment to come in sight of the frame work which surrounded the shaft. At length, after a long half hour, Tommy stumbled over an obstruction lying in a chamber which somehow seemed strangely familiar. He lifted his foot and gave the obstruction a hearty kick.

"That's my Indian sign of the trail!" grunted Sandy.

"For the love of Mike!" exclaimed Tommy. "Have we been traveling all this time to come out in this same old hole at last?"

"That's what we have!" replied Sandy. "If we had paid no attention to the string whatever and followed the rails when we came to the main gang way, we would have been home and in bed by this time!"

"But we didn't," grinned Tommy. "We thought we had a

cinch on getting out by way of this cord and so we followed that. I don't see, though," he continued, "how we came back to this same old chamber by following the cord. That looks queer to me!"

"I'll tell you how!" replied Sandy. "There's some gink been walking on ahead of us stringing the cord out for us to follow!"

Tommy sat down on the bottom of the chamber and wrinkled his freckled nose provokingly.

"We're a couple of easy marks!" he laughed.

"Easy marks is no name for it!"

"Well, what'll we do now to get out?" Tommy asked "First thing we know, it'll be daylight, and then Will and George'll be calling out the police to find us. We ought to get home before they wake up."

"I'm willing!" declared Sandy. "I'd like to be in my little bed this minute! I've had about enough of this foul air!"

The boys passed along until they came to the second trail sign and then stopped. Tommy pointed down to it with a hand which was not quite steady and looked up into his chum's face with frightened eyes.

"That's been moved!" he said.

"How do you know it's been moved?"

"Because you had the side stone on the other edge."

"I don't think I did!" argued Sandy.

The boys puzzled over the situation for a few moments, and then proceeded down the chamber looking for the tramway rails.

They passed from chamber to chamber and finally came to a place where the slope was upward.

"I guess we've struck it at last!" Sandy exclaimed.

"But there are no rails here!" Tommy argued.

"Then we're on the wrong track again," admitted Sandy.

He bent down to the rock with his searchlight and pointed out evidences that the passage had once been laid with rails.

"When they strip a chamber or a counter gangway," he said, "they take away the rails. It seems that we are now in a part of the Labyrinth mine which has been worked out."

"I know what to do!" exclaimed Tommy. "I'll give the call of the Beaver Patrol and tell those ginks who have been giving the call of the pack that we're lost! That ought to bring them out of their holes."

The Beaver call was given time after time, but no reply came.

"Say," Tommy said after his patience had become exhausted, "I believe it's daylight. Look at your watch. I left mine in the bed!"

"I left mine in bed, too," answered Sandy. "I know it is day, because I'm hungry."

CHAPTER IV

A SENSATIONAL DISCOVERY

When Will awoke he began preparations for breakfast before paying any attention whatever to his chums, whom he believed to be sleeping quietly on their cots. It was November, and quite chilly in the apartment, so his next efforts were directed to coaxing the electric coils into a cheery glow.

Presently George came tumbling out in his pyjamas and sat down on a rickety chair to talk of the adventures in prospect.

"I wonder if the Labyrinth mine is so much of a labyrinth after all?" he asked. "It seems to me that we might find our way through it without danger of losing ourselves," he continued with a yawn.

"It's some labyrinth, I take it," Will replied.

"Well, we can make chalk marks on the walls as we move along," suggested George. "Besides," he added, "we can string an electric wire through the center gangway and turn on the lights."

"There are probably electric lights there now," answered Will.

"Then there's no danger of our becoming lost," George argued.

"I wish you'd go to the back of the room and tip over those two cots," grinned Will. "It's the hardest kind of work to get Tommy and Sandy to bed, but when you do get them in bed once, it's harder still to get them out of it. Just tip the cots over and roll 'em out on the floor."

George approached the two cots in a stealthy manner and made ready to give Tommy and Sandy the bump of their lives.

"Don't break their necks!" advised Will.

As soon as George reached Tommy's bunk he stretched forth a hand for the purpose of tangling the boy up in the bedclothing so that his fall to the hard floor might be in a measure broken.

As he swung his hand over the cot, however, his eyes widened and he called out to Will that the boys were not in their cots.

There was a look of alarm as well as of annoyance on each face as the lads thought over the situation.

"The little idiots!" exclaimed Will.

"That isn't strong enough!" George corrected.

"There's no knowing how long they've been gone," Will suggested. "The chances are that they went away as soon as we went to sleep."

"In that case, they're in trouble!" George declared.

V. T. Sherman

"In what kind of trouble?"

"The good Lord only knows!" replied George. "Tommy and Sandy can get into more different kinds of trouble in less time than any other boys on the face of the earth. They're the original lookers for trouble!"

"Do you suppose they've got lost in the mine?" asked Will.

"It may be worse than that!" cried George. "They may have butted into some of the people the caretaker indirectly referred to last night."

"He did speak of strange noises and mysterious lights, didn't he?"

"He certainly did, and I've got a hunch that Sandy and Tommy have butted into some hostile interests.

"It does seem as if they would be back by this time unless they were in trouble!"

The boys prepared an elaborate breakfast in the hope that Tommy and Sandy, who would be sure to be hungry, would return in time to partake of it. A dozen times during the meal they walked back to the shaft opening and looked anxiously down into the dark bowels of the mine.

"Those fellows are always getting into trouble," Will said, rather crossly, as he stood looking down. "They have a way of running into most of their dangers at night, too. It was the same up on Lake Superior; the same in the snake-haunted Everglades of Florida; the same on the Rocky Mountains, and the same in the Hudson Bay country."

"They sure do keep things moving," grinned George.

"I think," Will suggested after a time, "that we'd better find Canfield and get his advice before we do anything in the way of setting up a search. I hate to admit that two members of our party got into a scrape on the same night we struck the mine, but I guess there's no way out of it."

While the boys talked together, the door opened softly and the caretaker entered, accompanied by a short, paunchy man with a very red face and eyes which were black, small and suspicious. He was a man well past middle age, but he seemed to be making a bluff at thirty-five. His hair, which had turned white at the temples, and his moustache were both dyed black.

Canfield introduced the new-comer as the detective, Joe Ventner, of New York, and the boys greeted him courteously.

He accepted their proffered hands with an air of condescension which was most exasperating. He puffed out his chest, and at once began talking of some of his alleged exploits in the secret service of the government.

"How did you pass the night, boys?" asked the caretaker.

"Slept like pigs!" replied Will with a laugh.

"Where are the others?" asked Canfield.

"They're out getting a breath of fresh air, I reckon," answered George.

The boys did not take to the detective at all. There was an air of insincerity about the man which at once put them on their guard.

Had Canfield visited them alone, they would have explained to him the exact situation. In the presence of this detective, however, they decided to do nothing of the kind.

"Now then," the detective said after a moment's silence, "if you boys will outline the course you intend to pursue in this matter, I think we can manage to work together without our plans clashing."

"We have talked the matter over during the night," Will replied, "and have decided to remain here only long enough to obtain some clue as to the direction taken by the boys in their departure."

"Then you think they are not here?" asked the detective.

"There is no reason why they should be here, is there?" asked Will.

"I don't know that there is," relied Ventner.

"Can you imagine any reason for their wanting to linger about the mine?" asked George.

"No," was the reply. "It has always been my opinion that the boys left the mine because they feared arrest for some boyish offense committed in some other part of the country, and that they are now far away from this place."

Both lads observed that the detective seemed particularly pleased with the statement that they proposed to abandon the search of the mine immediately. Somehow, they caught the impression that they would interfere with his plans if they remained.

"It might be well," Ventner said, directly, "to keep me posted as to any discoveries you may make. We must work together, you know."

"Certainly," replied Will, speaking with a mental reservation which did not include the giving up of any information worth while.

"Well, then, I'll be going," the detective said, strutting across the room, with his little round belly protruding like that of an insect. "You can always find me at the hotel down here, if I'm in this part of the country. Just ask for me and I'll show up."

Canfield was turning to depart with the detective when Will motioned to him to remain. The caretaker turned back with a surprised look.

Will waited until the door had closed on the detective before speaking. Even then, he went to the door and glanced down the passage.

"Something exciting?" smiled the caretaker, noting the boy's caution.

"Yes," Will answered, "there's something exciting. Tommy and Sandy disappeared during the night."

"Disappeared?" echoed the caretaker.

"Yes," George cut in, "there was some talk of their visiting the mine just before we went to bed, and we are of the opinion that they went down the shaft shortly after we fell asleep, and failed to find their way to the surface again. We are considerably alarmed."

"I should think you would be!" replied the caretaker. "In the first place, the Labyrinth mine bears the right name. There are old workings below which a stranger might follow for days without finding the way out."

"Then we'll have to organize a search for the boys," George suggested.

"Besides," continued Canfield, "there are things going on in the mine which no one understands. I have long believed that there are people living there who have no right to take up such a residence."

"I'm sorry you said anything to this detective about our being here," Will said, after this phase of the case had been discussed.

"As a matter of fact," the caretaker replied, "I didn't intend to say anything to Ventner about your being here, but in some way he received an intimation that you were about to take up the case and so pumped the whole story out of me."

"Perhaps he received his information from the New York attorney," suggested Will.

"I'm sure that he did not," answered the caretaker. "If the attorney had written to him in regard to the matter at all, he would have posted him so fully that when he cross-examined me such a proceeding would have been unnecessary."

"Has this man Ventner visited the mine often?" asked George.

"Yes, quite frequently."

"Does he always go alone?"

"Yes, he always goes alone," was the answer. "Once I accompanied him to the bottom of the shaft, but there he suggested that we go in different directions, and did not seem to want me anywhere near him."

"I don't like the looks of the fellow, and that's a fact!" exclaimed Will. "He doesn't look good to me."

After some discussion it was decided that the caretaker would accompany the two boys to the bottom of the shaft and direct them down gangways, which they could follow without fear of losing their way, and the illumination of which would be likely to be observed by anyone wandering about the blind chambers and passages of the mine.

When they reached the bottom of the shaft, climbing down the ladders, as Tommy and Sandy had done some hours before, they gathered in a little group at the bottom while the caretaker gave them a few general instructions regarding the general outlines of the Labyrinth of tunnels, chambers and cross passages which lay before them.

"Did any one come down after us?" asked Will directly.

"No one," was the reply. "Why do you ask?"

"Because," Will answered, "there's some one skulking off down that passage, and it looks to me like that bum detective!"

CHAPTER V

THE FLOODED MINE

"What makes you think it's Ventner?" asked the caretaker. "Did you see his face? I don't think he is here."

"I didn't see his face," answered Will, "but I saw the shape of his shoulders and the hang-dog look of him."

"You're prejudiced against Ventner," laughed Canfield.

"I admit it!" replied Will. "He looks to me like a snake in the grass. I don't think anything he could do would look good to me."

"Now," Canfield said, "perhaps we'd better be mapping out a plan of campaign. Here are three gangways leading in three different directions. We'll leave one of the lights burning at the shaft, then we'll each take a light and proceed into the interior, making as much noise as we conveniently can, and flashing the light into all the chambers and cross headings we come to."

"How long are these gangways?" asked Will.

"Somewhere near a half a mile straight ahead!" was the answer.

The caretaker went away swinging his electric searchlight, and Will and George pushed forward in their respective passages.

After proceeding a short distance, George heard Will calling to him.

"There's some one just ahead of me in the gangway!" Will declared. "I think we ought to go together!"

"Do you think it's that bum detective?" asked George.

"I certainly do!"

"Well, we can go together if you like," George said. "We can't cover quite as much ground in that way, but I guess we can accomplish more in the long run!"

The boys had proceeded only a short distance when they heard Canfield calling to them. A moment later they heard the caretaker's steps ringing on the hard floor of the gangway down which they were advancing. He came up to them panting, in a moment.

"There's something mighty queer about this mine," the caretaker declared. "It was punk dry only two days ago, and now there are four or five feet of water where the gangway I started to follow dips down.

"And look there!" Will exclaimed holding his light aloft and pointing, "you can see plenty of water ahead! I guess all the gangways are taking a washing, and the water seems to be rising, too!"

"Is there any way by which the mine could be intentionally flooded?" asked George. "There may be some one planning trouble for the owners."

"There is only one way that I know of in which the mine could be flooded intentionally," replied the caretaker. "There is a large drain, of course, in what is known as the sump. Considerable water runs off in that way, and the rest of the drippings are taken out by the pumps. If this sump drainage should become clogged, the mine, of course, would become flooded though not to such an extent, unless the pumps were kept constantly at work."

"Then I guess you'd better set the pumps going," Will suggested. "We can't get into the mine in its present condition unless we swim."

"Haven't you got a boat?" asked George.

"Why, yes," replied the caretaker. "There's a couple of boats somewhere in the mine. The operators placed them here thinking they might come in handy at some future time, but I haven't any idea where they are now. Still, I think they're not far away."

"If you'll go and set the pumps in motion," Will advised, "George and I'll look around for the boats. We may need them before the pumps get under motion the way the water is pouring in now."

"I guess Tommy and Sandy don't come back because they're penned in by water," George suggested, as the boys began searching the vicinity of the shaft for the boats.

"If they're anywhere within hearing distance, they ought to answer us when we called out, hadn't they?" asked Will.

"We haven't tried that yet," George answered. "Suppose we

let out a couple of yells!"

To think in this case was to act, and the boys did let out a couple of yells which brought the caretaker running back from the shaft.

The boys were listening for some answer to their shouts when he arrived, and so they paid little attention to his numerous questions.

"There is no time to lose," Canfield went on. "I'll go to the top at once and call an engineer and a couple of firemen. When you find the boat, take a trip down the main gangway here and stick your lights into all the crossheadings and chambers you see. But, above all," he continued, "don't fail to leave a light here at a shaft, and be careful that you never pass out of sight of it."

Canfield hastened away, climbing the ladders two rungs at a time, and soon disappeared into the little dot of light at the top.

The two boys searched patiently for the boat for a long time, but did not succeed in discovering it. At last, Will suggested that it might be in the mule stable and thither they went.

The boat was there, in excellent condition, and the boys soon had it swinging to and fro on the surface of the water which now lay several feet deep in the main gangway.

"Je-rusalem!" exclaimed George, taking the depth of the water with an oar, "if the water is four feet deep here, how deep must it be at the middle of the dip?"

"About forty rods, I should think!" exaggerated Will.

V. T. Sherman

The boys left a large searchlight at the shaft, so situated that it looked straight down the passage they proposed following, and started away in the boat. The flashlights illuminated only a small portion of the underground place, but the boys could see some distance straight ahead.

Once they ceased rowing to listen, believing that they had heard calls from the darkness beyond. The sound was not repeated, and they were about to proceed when a sound which brought all their nervous energy into full swing reached their ears.

It was the bumping of an oar or paddle against the side of a boat. The blow echoed through the cavern as sharply as a pistol shot might have done. There could be no mistake in the cause.

"Now who's in that other boat?"

"Somehow," George grumbled in a whisper, "we always have propositions like that put up to us! There's always a mystery in every trip we take! We found one on Lake Superior, and one in the Florida Everglades, and one at the top of the Rocky mountains and one in the Hudson Bay wilderness."

"Yes, and we solved them, too!" grinned Will. "And we're going to solve this one! You remember about my seeing some one sneaking in here just ahead of us, don't you?"

"Yes," was the answer. "You thought it was that bum detective."

"I think so yet," replied Will.

"If it's the detective," asked George, "why didn't he give the alarm when he found that the mine was being flooded. He might at least have done that and saved the company a great deal of expense and trouble."

"Give it up," replied Will. "I might ask you," he went on, "why he was rowing away into a flooded mine which is supposed to be deserted."

"And I'd have to give you the answer you gave me," George declared.

The boys could now hear the strokes of the oarsman who was in the lead quite regularly and distinctly. Now and then he turned into crossheadings and chambers, as if to escape from their surveillance, but they kept steadily on after him, not taking into account the fact that they were leaving the light they had set at the shaft far out of view.

"Perhaps we ought to turn back now," George proposed, in a short time, seeing that they came no nearer to the boat in advance. "We left the main gangway some time ago, and we ought not to get too far away from it."

Will turned and looked back, facing only an inky blackness.

"We should have stuck to the main gangway," he said. "I don't even remember when we left it! Is it very far back?"

"Some distance," answered George. "You see we followed this other boat without thinking what we were doing."

"Perhaps, if we continue to follow the other boat, it will lead us somewhere. The fellow rowing must know something about the interior of the mine or he probably wouldn't be here!"

"I've been listening for a minute or more, trying to catch sound of the fellow's oars," George went on, "but there's nothing doing. I guess he's led us into a blind chamber and slipped away!"

"We don't seem to be lacking for excitement," Will suggested with a grin. "We've lost Tommy and Sandy, and the machinery of the mine has been interfered with, and the lower levels are filling with water! Any old time we start out to do things, there's a general mixup!"

"Aw, quit growling and listen a minute," suggested George.

The boys listened only for a moment when the sound George had heard was repeated. It was the call of the Wolf pack!

CHAPTER VI

THE BEAVER CALL

"That's Tommy!" exclaimed Will.

"I never knew that he belonged to the Wolf Patrol!" George observed.

"He might give the call without belonging to the Patrol!" urged Will.

The boys listened, but the sound was not repeated, although they called out the names of their chums and gave the Beaver call repeatedly.

"I guess it was a dream," George suggested.

"Then it was the most vivid dream I ever had!" Will declared.

They rowed about the chamber for some moments searching for the source of the call, but to no purpose.

"Let's go back to the shaft," urged George.

"I'm agreeable," answered Will. "The only question now is

whether we can find the shaft. The water is so deep that all branches of the mine look alike to me!"

In passing out of the chamber into another passage the boys were obliged to stoop low in order to avoid what is called a dip.

After passing under the dip so close to the ceiling that the boys were obliged to lie down in the boat in order to protect their heads, they came to a large chamber which seemed to be fairly dry save in the center, where there was a depression of considerable size.

"Nothing doing here!" Will exclaimed as he flashed his searchlight around the place. "This chamber looks as if there hadn't been an ounce of coal mined here for a hundred years."

"Then let's get out," George proposed, "and make our way back to the shaft if possible. If we can't, we'll make noise enough to attract Canfield's attention and let him come and lead us out."

"Here we go, then," cried Will, giving the boat a great push toward the dip. "We can't get out any too fast."

The boat came up against a solid projection of rock!

"I don't seem to see any way out!" George exclaimed.

"Well, it's there somewhere!" declared Will.

"I see it now!" cried George. "It's under water!"

"Under water?" repeated Will.

"Yes, under water!" answered George. "If we don't get out of this hole before the pumps get to working we'll have to swim!"

Will turned his searchlight on the dip and saw that it was now full clear to the down dropping roof.

"I guess we'll have to swim," he agreed.

"That black water doesn't look good to me," George exclaimed with a little shudder. "It seems to me that I can see snakes and alligators wiggling in it from here. Looks worse to me than the swamps of the Everglades! And there was a quart of snakes to every pint of water down there!"

"But we got to swim just the same!" urged Will. "In half an hour from now the air in this chamber will be unbreathable. There is no vent at all, now that the water fills the dip, and the coal gas is naturally seeping in all the time."

"That's all right, too!" admitted George. "But I'm not going to jump into that black water until I have to. If a rope or something should twine around my legs while I was in there, I'd drop dead with fright! Besides," he went on, "the chances are that Canfield will get the pumps going before long now."

The boys waited for a long half hour, during which time the water rose steadily. It seemed certain that the mine was about to be flooded throughout all the lower levels.

"Tommy and Sandy may have bumped into just such a situation as this," Will said, as he pushed the boat from side to side in the hope of coming upon some exit from the place.

"Serves 'em good and right!" exclaimed George.

Will chuckled to himself and held a wet hand high up toward the roof of the chamber or passage.

"There's a current of air here!" he said.

"Then we won't smother to death!" George grunted.

"And, look here," Will continued, as the boat bumped into a pyramid of shale which had been thrown up to within a few inches of the roof, "some one has been building this hill of refuse and using it for a refuge!"

"It does look that way," George agreed. "That shows that at some time the water must have ascended to the very top of the wall. We may have to climb up there ourselves in order to keep from getting our clothing soaked in that ink down there!"

The water rose higher and higher in the passage, and it seemed to the boys that by this time most of the lower gangways were entirely impassible.

"It doesn't seem to me that the water in this blooming old mine could rise any faster if the whole Mississippi river were turned into it!" cried George in a tone of disgust. "If Canfield doesn't get his pumps going before long, he'll have a job here that'll take him all winter!"

"I presume he's doing the best he can," Will argued. "For all we know, the boilers as well as the electric motors may have been tampered with. That would be just our luck!"

"I wonder what's become of that bum detective?" asked George after a short silence. "We heard him rowing along in front of us one minute, and the next minute there wasn't a single sound to indicate that there was another boat in the mine."

"As soon as I get out of this," Will stated, "I'm going to make it my business to find out whether that detective is regularly employed on this case. He looks to me like a crook!"

It was dreary waiting there in the sealed-up chamber, and the boys found themselves dropping into long intervals of silence while they listened for the gurgle of the water which would indicate that the great pumps had been set in motion.

During one of those intervals of silence, they heard sounds which brought them to their feet in great excitement. Almost unable to believe his ears, Will turned to George with a question on his lips:

"Did you hear that?" he asked.

"Of course I did!"

"I did, too, but I thought I must be dreaming."

"No dream about that!" replied George. "That's the call of the Beaver Patrol!"

"And that means that Tommy and Sandy are not far away!"

"We heard the call of the Wolf Patrol not long ago," suggested George. "I wonder if this blooming old mine is chock full of Boy Scouts of assorted sizes. There can't be too many here to please me!"

The boys returned the Beaver call but no answer came. At times they thought they heard whispers coming from the dark reaches of the cavern, but they were not quite certain.

"There may be real Beavers in here for all we know!" suggested Will.

V. T. Sherman

"That's all you know about it!" chuckled George. "Beavers only operate in running water."

"Well, isn't that water out there running?" asked Will.

"No jokes now!" replied George. "I've got all I can endure now without standing for any of your alleged witticisms!"

While the boys sat in the boat, occasionally moving it from side to side, a shaft of light appeared directly above the point where the shale had been heaped up. It moved swiftly about for an instant and then dropped out of view. It was a moment before either boy spoke.

"That's some of Tommy's foolishness!" Will declared.

George repeated the Beaver call several times, but no answer came.

"That's a searchlight, anyway!" insisted Will. "And I don't believe these ginks in the mines have electric searchlights to lug around with them!"

Will unshipped an oar and struck the water with the flat of the blade several times, exerting his whole strength.

"Keep it up!" advised George. "That sounds exactly like a beaver's tail connecting with the surface of a stream!"

"Yes, keep it up!" cried a voice out of the darkness. "Keep it up, and perhaps some beaver'll come along and build a dam to get you out of that mess you're in! You're always getting into trouble, you two!"

"You've got your nerve with you!" exclaimed Will, half-angrily. "Here you go out in the night and get lost, and we come out after you, and the mine gets flooded, and we get tied up between the solid wall and a bend in the passage, and then you blame us for getting into trouble!"

"Can you climb?" chuckled Tommy, throwing the rays of his searchlight on the boat. "If you can, just mount up on that pile of shale and work your way through the opening between the two levels. This might have been used as a sort of an air hole a few hundred years ago," he went on, "but I'll bet that not one out of a hundred of the miners of today know that there is an opening here!"

Leaving the boat, the boys mounted the pile of shale and were soon making their way up the rugged face of the shaft in the direction of the level, which ran along above the one now being flooded.

"Can you find your way out of this dump, now?" asked Will as the boys stood with their chums at the end of a long passage.

CHAPTER VII

A TREACHEROUS FOE

"There seems to be fewer twists and turns in this level than on the one below it," Tommy explained, "and I guess we can find our way out readily enough. If we don't," he went on, "I shall be obliged to eat a ton or two of coal to keep from starving to death."

"Serves you right!" declared Will. "You had no business getting up in the middle of the night and wandering off into the mine!"

"What did you do?" demanded Tommy.

"We waited until morning, and then enlisted the services of the caretaker," replied Will. "So far as I can remember, this is about the nine hundredth relief expedition we've been out on in search of you boys!"

"Seems to me," Tommy chuckled, "that you're the lads that were in need of the relief expedition! We found you boxed up in a chamber in a boat."

"But we wouldn't have been in any such mess if we hadn't started out to look you up!" George declared.

"We should have been back before you got out of bed this morning, if some one hadn't cut our string," replied Sandy. "We had a cinch on getting out, but some geezer led us a fool chase by cutting our cord and steering us around in a circle."

"Did you see any one?" asked Will.

"Not a soul!" was the reply. "But there's some one in here, just the same. We heard the call of the Wolf Patrol a long time ago and we've heard it several times since."

"What do you mean by some one cutting your string?" asked George.

"Why," replied Sandy, "we tied the loose end of a ball of twine to one of the shaft timbers and unwound the ball as we moved along, expecting to follow it back when we wanted to get out."

"How do you know some one cut it?" asked Will.

"Perhaps you broke it," George suggested.

Sandy took a piece of the cord from his pocket and passed it over to George with a sly chuckle.

"See if you can break that!" he said.

George tried his best to break the string, but it remained firm under all his strength.

The boys now fell into a discussion of the ways and means of getting out of the mine.

"I believe," Sandy exclaimed, "that if we follow the current of air which the rising water is forcing out of this old shaft, we will come to the entrance. As you all know, a current of air takes the shortest way to any given point, and this one ought to blow straight toward the shaft."

"Great head, that, little boy!" laughed Tommy.

After proceeding some distance the steady thud, thud of the pumping machinery was heard, and the boys understood that the efforts of the caretaker were at last bringing results. The sounds also aided them in direction, and in a short time they stood at the shaft on the second level.

When they came out to the timber work, Will, who was in the lead, motioned to the others to remain in the background.

"What's doing now?" whispered Sandy.

"There's a man working on the ladders," explained Will in a low whisper. "I can't see him yet, but I can hear the sound of a saw."

"He may be cutting the rungs," suggested Tommy.

"That's the notion I had," replied Will. "Suppose we all get around behind the air shaft and wait until we can find out what he is up to. It may be that bum detective, for all we know."

"What would he be doing there?" questioned Sandy.

"Sawing the rungs!" whispered Will. "He wouldn't cut them down, of course, but he might saw them so that they would break under our weight and give us a drop of a couple of hundred feet."

"It doesn't seem as if any human being would do a thing like that!" cried George. "It would be a wicked thing to do!"

While the boys whispered together, the sound of sawing continued. The man engaged at the task was evidently unfamiliar with such work, for they heard him puffing and blowing as the saw cut through the wood.

"He's cutting the rungs, all right!" Will said in a moment. "And that cuts off our escape until the cables can be put in motion and the cages started. I wish I had him by the neck!"

"We'll get him by the neck, all right, before many days," Sandy cut in, "if we can only get a sight of him so as to be sure of his identity."

Presently the man ceased working, and they heard him ascending the ladders, step by step. In a moment the saw which he had been using dropped from his hands and clattered to the bottom of the shaft.

Then they heard him springing swiftly forward, and directly they knew that he had reached the top. The boys all looked disgusted.

"And we never caught sight of him!" exclaimed Tommy.

Will now walked around to the front of the shaft and looked down. The saw which had been used lay shining on the lower level.

"I'm going down after that!" he said in a moment.

"Yes, you are!" whispered Tommy.

"Got to have it!" insisted Will.

"Well, go on and get it, then," laughed Sandy. "You've got to show me!"

"I don't think he cut the rungs between this level and the next one," George interposed. "It may be safe to use the lower ladders."

"I can soon find out!" Will declared.

The cutting had been done between the second level and the top. The ladders below seemed perfectly safe. After testing them thoroughly, Will trusted himself on one of the rungs and let himself down slowly, bearing as much weight as was possible on the standards.

He was at the bottom in a moment, and in another moment stood by the side of his chums with the saw in his hand.

"I don't think that's so very much!" Tommy exclaimed.

"Right here, then," Will explained, "is where you get your little Sherlock Holmes lesson! This is a new saw, as you all see. It probably never was used before. Now the man who did the cutting bought this at some nearby store. Don't you see what it means?"

"That's a fact!" cried Tommy. "We can find out who bought the saw, and so discover the gink who tried to commit murder by sawing the ladders."

"And look here," Will went on, "do you see these threads hanging to the teeth of the saw? Do you see the color?"

"Blue!" replied the boys in a breath.

"That's right, blue. Now, what sort of a suit did the detective wear this morning? It was blue, wasn't it?"

"Sure it was!" replied George. "A blue serge! I noticed it particularly because it wasn't much of a fit."

"Well, these are blue serge threads!" commented Will.

"That's right, too," admitted Sandy.

While the boys still stood at the second level they heard some one moving down from the top. Will rushed around to the ladder and looked up.

He could not see the face of the man who was climbing down, but he could see that he did not wear a blue serge suit.

In a moment he called out to him, asking some trivial question regarding the action of the pumps. When the man looked down he saw that it was Canfield. The caretaker seemed surprised at finding the boys at the second level. He kept on descending.

"Wait!" Will called. "Stop where you are!"

"But I've got to find out what's the matter with the machinery at the bottom," the caretaker called out. "There's something wrong there!"

"Then you'd better take long steps," replied Will, "for if you put any weight on those rungs, you're likely to land at the bottom of the shaft. The rungs have been cut!"

"I can't believe that!" replied Canfield.

"Suppose you look and see!"

The caretaker advanced cautiously downward until he came to where a fine line of sawdust lay on one of the rungs.

"Do you know who did this?" he asked.

"We think we do," replied Will, "but this isn't any time for long stories. The first thing for us to do is to get back into the breaker and cook Tommy and Sandy three or four breakfasts apiece!"

"So you found them, did you?" asked Canfield.

"No; we found them," shouted Tommy.

"Well, how're you going to get out?" asked the caretaker.

"Get a rope," directed Will, "and throw it over the sound rung lowest down, and we'll climb up until we can trust our weight on the ladder."

This plan was followed, and in a short time the boys all stood, hungry and tired, in their room in the breaker. Tommy made an instantaneous dive for the provisions which had been brought in the night before.

"Nice old time we've had!" he exclaimed, with his mouth full of pork and beans. "I guess we're some Boy Scouts after all!"

"I'm going to tie you up tonight!" Will declared.

While the boys talked and ate the caretaker darted to the door leading to the passage which ended at the shaft.

He returned in a moment looking both angry and frightened.

"The pumps have stopped!" he said. "The mine will probably

be flooded before tomorrow morning! The very devil seems to have taken full charge here today. I never saw anything like it!"

"There are boys in the mine who will be drowned!" exclaimed Tommy.

"I'm not so sure of that!" answered Canfield. "It was only a suggestion on my part that the boys we are in search of have taken refuge under ground. I think I must have been mistaken!"

"Do you know whether these breaker boys belonged to the Boy Scouts or not?" asked Will. "Did you ever see any medals or badges on their clothing which told of Boy Scout experiences?"

"Sure they belong to the Boy Scouts!" declared the caretaker, "and that is the very reason why I sent for Boy Scouts to help find them."

"What Patrol did they belong to?" asked Will.

"If you had heard them howling like wolves around the breaker night after night," was the reply, "you wouldn't ask what patrol they belonged to!"

"Then they are in the mine!" shouted Tommy. "We all heard the call of the pack, but the funny thing is that they wouldn't show themselves."

V. T. Sherman

CHAPTER VIII

"THEY WENT UP IN THE AIR!"

"There's something funny-about those boys!" exclaimed Canfield. "They seemed to be merry-hearted fellows, just a little bit full of mischief, but for some reason they never mixed with the others much."

"Where did they come from when they came here?" asked Will.

"The information in the letters I received from the attorney in charge of the case is that they came here from New York, not directly but by some round-about way."

"Did this attorney ever inform you why he wanted the boys found?" asked Tommy. "Are we all working in the dark?"

"He never told me why he wanted the boys found. For all I know, they may be wanted for some crime, or they may be heirs to an immense property. My instructions are to find them. That's all!"

"Where did these boys lodge?" asked Will.

"They didn't have any regular room," was the reply. "They

slept in the breaker whenever the watchman would permit them to do so, and when he wouldn't, they threw stones at him and slept in the railroad yard somewhere. But the strangest part of the whole business is the way they disappeared from sight."

"You didn't tell us about that!" exclaimed Sandy.

"I meant to," the caretaker answered. "The last seen of them here they were at work on the breaker. It was somewhere near the middle of the afternoon, and the cracker boss had been particularly ugly. The two boys were often caught whispering together, and more than once the cracker boss had launched such trifles as half pound blocks of shale at them. I happened to be on the outside just about that time."

"The boys didn't go up in the air, did they?" asked Sandy with a chuckle. "They haven't got wings, have they?"

"To all intents and purposes, they went up into the air!" answered the caretaker. "One moment they were on the breaker sorting slate and stuff of that kind out of the stream of coal which was pouring down upon them, and the next moment they were nowhere in sight!"

"Had any strangers been seen talking with them?"

"Now you come to a point that I should have mentioned before!" replied the caretaker. "Two days before they left a strange boy came to the mine and went to work on the breaker. He was an unusually well-mannered, well-dressed young fellow, and so the breaker boys called him a dude. He resented this, of course, and there was a fight at the first quitting time. These two boys, Jimmie and Dick, stood by the new lad, and gave three or four of the tough little chaps who work on the breaker a good beating up."

"Now we've got hold of something!" exclaimed Will. "Were these three boys together much after that?"

"No," was the reply. "The new boy thanked Jimmie and Dick for helping him through his scrape, and that was about all. They might have talked together for five minutes that night, but they were never seen, in each other's company again so far as I know."

"How long did this new boy stay here?" asked George.

"He quit the next day."

"He didn't go up in a pillar of fire, did he?" grinned Sandy.

"No, he walked up to the office and asked if he could get his pay for the time he had worked. The boss told him he'd have to wait until Saturday night, and he turned up his nose and walked out."

"And where did he go?" asked George.

"He said he was going down the river in a boat," answered the caretaker. "He bought an old boat, stocked it with quite a supply of provisions, and started on his way. The next day the boat was found bottom side up on a bar, and the lad's hat lay on the bank not far away."

"Do you think he was drowned?" asked Sandy.

"It would seem so."

"Drowned nothing!" exclaimed Tommy. "He sneaked those provisions into the mine under cover of the darkness, and the three little rascals are feeding on them yet. You can see the end of that without a telescope!"

"Now, smarty!" exclaimed George. "You've told us where the boys went, and where the provisions landed, and all that, now tell us why these kids hid themselves in the mine. And while you are about it, you may as well tell why they gave the Wolf call and refused to reply."

"This story," replied Tommy with a grin, "is not a novelette, complete in one number. It's a serial story, and will be continued in our next issue. What did you say about the pumps stopping, Mr. Canfield?"

"They've stopped, all right!" the caretaker replied.

"Are you going to let the ginks flood the mine?" asked Sandy.

"While I was out a few moments ago," Canfield explained, "I notified one of the clerks in the company's office to send up a gang of men to repair the machinery. They ought to be here by this time."

"How long will it take to repair the pump?" asked Tommy.

"It may take an hour and it may take twenty-four."

"In the meantime," Tommy continued, "do you think you could send one of the county officers out to round up this bum detective?"

"You mean that you want him watched?" asked Canfield.

"Sure!" answered Tommy. "He sawed the rungs in the shaft, didn't he? He could get ten years for that!"

"All right," replied Canfield. "I'll send word out and have him arrested if you are positive that he is the man that did the cutting."

"We are positive that he's the man," replied Will, "but it'll spoil everything if you have him arrested. We want to give him a free hand for a time, and see what he will do. He's a crook, and he's bound to show it! And another thing," the boy went on, "we don't want anyone to know that he is under suspicion. We just want him watched."

"You're handling the case," smiled Canfield, "and I'll take any steps you advise. I can't tell you how sorry I am that I brought the detective in here this morning!"

"Well," Will said, "we put up a bluff about getting out of town and perhaps we can make that stick. We can take a train out and come back in on a lonely freight, and get into the mine without his knowing anything about it. The mine is the best place to work from, anyway!"

"That's why I wanted to know how soon the mine could be pumped out!" stated Tommy. "I don't care about wading around in a mess of water that's blacker than a stack of black cats."

"I think I can have the mine fairly dry by the time you boys get out of town and back again!" laughed Canfield.

"Well," Tommy said, "then you'd better get a couple of dry-goods boxes and fill them full of good things to eat, and drop 'em down to the first level. Perhaps you know of a cosy little chamber there where we can set up housekeeping."

"I know just the place," said the caretaker. "To the left of the old tool house there's a room where odd articles of every description have been stored for any number of years. The blacksmith and the fire-boss used to go there to smoke and tell stories, if I remember right."

"Does anyone ever go there now?" asked Will.

"Not that I know of," was the reply.

"Then we'll drop down there some time towards morning," Will decided. "And in the meantime," he added, with a wink at his chums, "we'll be looking for a boy tramp out in the railroad yards."

"What do you mean by that?" asked the caretaker.

"Oh, I've just got an idea," replied Will, "that there's a kid hanging around this part of the country whom we ought to interview."

"But I don't understand."

"You wait until we get hold of him, and you'll understand all right!" laughed Will. "We just need that boy!"

"But how do you know there is such a boy?" urged the caretaker.

"He gets it out of a dream book!" Tommy chuckled.

"Do you mean to say that there is some go-between between the boys who may or may not be in the mine and some persons outside who are interested in them?" asked the caretaker.

"I didn't say anything of the kind!" replied Will.

"There are times," Tommy explained to Canfield, "when the gift of frank speech is taken away from Will, so you mustn't blame him for not answering. He'll tell you all about it when the time comes."

The caretaker went away with a puzzled look on his honest face.

CHAPTER IX

WHO DISCOVERED THE LEAK?

"You've got to explanation me," George laughed, as the caretaker left the room, and the boys began picking up their clothing, preparatory to the alleged journey. "I can't understand what you mean by saying that you'll watch out for a boy tramp in the railroad yards."

"It's a sure thing, isn't it?" Will asked, "that the boys we are in search of are in the mine? We don't know what they're in there for. They may be hiding there because of some fool notion they have in their heads, or they may have been sent here for some definite purpose."

"You bet they've been sent here for some definite purpose," George replied. "They never came here to work on the breaker without having some well-defined motive. Boys answering to their description don't accept such jobs as they accepted here!"

"Well, the boys are in the mine," Will continued. "As stated, we don't know what they're there for, but we know they're there. Now, this third boy comes to the mine and works just long enough to get in touch with the other two. Then he disappears."

V. T. Sherman

"Buys a lot of provisions and goes down the river to leave his hat on the bank!" laughed Tommy. "I guess that was a pretty poor imitation of a suicide or a drowning accident, either!"

"But this boy didn't get to be intimate with the two breaker boys," contended George. "He talked with them about two minutes after the fight, according to Canfield, but paid no further attention to them after that. If he had any secret understanding with them, he must have done a whole lot of talking in a mighty short space of time."

"The right kind of a boy can say a good deal in a minute and half!" laughed Tommy. "But suppose we let Will go on and explanation us about that boy tramp in the railroad yards. I think I know what he's getting at, but I'm not quite certain. Go on, Will, it's up to you."

"In order to make the connection," laughed Will. "I'll state for the third time that we know that the boys are in the mine. It may also be well to state, once more, that we are reasonably certain that this third boy came to the mine for the specific purpose of communicating with the other two. Now, this boy didn't drop into the river. He dropped the provisions he bought for the boat into the coal mine, and left them there for the consumption of the two boys inside. That's reasonable, isn't it?"

"Fine deduction, as Sherlock Holmes would say to Watson!" laughed George.

"But this third boy," Will went on, "doesn't go into the mine. He stays outside to serve as a means of communication between the boys who are hiding in the mine and some interested person or persons on the outside. That's perfectly clear, isn't it?"

"That'll do very well for a theory," replied George.

"I'll go you a plate of cookies," argued Sandy, "that Will is right, and that this third boy is hanging around taking messages from the two boys in the mine and also to the two boys in the mine."

"Didn't I say it was all right for a theory?" chuckled George.

"Now, the point is this," Will continued. "What are those boys in the mine for? What do they want there? Why didn't they answer our Boy Scout challenge when we replied to their call of the pack?"

"If you don't ask so many questions, you won't get so many negative answers," Sandy advised. "We're here to find the boys, and I don't see that it makes any difference to us what they're in there for."

"But we've found the boys now," contended Tommy. "We haven't got our hands on them yet, of course, but we know they're in there, and we know it's only a question of time when we get hold of them."

"Well," Will insisted, "I'm going to find a motive before I quit the case. I'm going to know who sent those boys here, and all about it, before I make any report to Mr. Horton."

"Go as far as you like," laughed Tommy. "My bump of curiosity is growing half an inch a day, and will continue to spread out until I find out exactly what those boys are doing burrowing in a deserted mine."

"Now, we'll get back to the point we started from," Will explained. "This boy who is undoubtedly doing duty outside the mine in the interests of the persons who sent the two boys in, furnishes the clue to the whole situation! When we find him, and find out what he's up to, and trace any communications he may make back to their original source, we'll have the whole case tied up tight!"

"That's right!" declared Tommy. "We'll have the case tied up tight if we succeed in getting hold of this third boy."

"Oh, go on!" laughed Sandy. "We'll be picking third boys and fourth boys and fifth boys out of the air, first thing you know. We never went away on a Boy Scout expedition yet that we didn't find all manner of kids hanging around on purpose to be discovered. We found them on Old Superior; and in the Everglades; and on the Great Continental Divide; and up in the Hudson Bay country, we began to think we had stumbled on the center of population so far as Boy Scouts were concerned!"

"There's just one thing that's likely to make us trouble," Will resumed. "And that is the fact that Canfield very foolishly slopped over to Ventner when explaining the purpose of our visit here. That bum detective knows now that we're here to search the mine. Of course he might have received, as Canfield says, the most of his information from outside sources, but the caretaker should have thrown him off the track instead of telling him exactly what our mission here was."

"But Ventner came here to search for the boys himself!" George broke in. "At least, he says that he did."

"There's a mystery about the whole matter," Sandy declared, "and I'd like to help clear it up from beginning to end!"

"We're likely to have a chance!" laughed Tommy.

"What are we going to do all the afternoon?" George asked.

"Wander around town," smiled Will, "and find out about the evening train, and ask fool questions about the pumps and the mine, and laugh at the idea of anybody living in there. That'll give Ventner the idea that we're going for good, I reckon. He's a pretty bum skate to pose as a detective!"

"I'll tell you what I'm going to do most of the afternoon!" Tommy declared. "I'm going to the hay! I never felt so bunged up for want of sleep in my innocent life."

"Haven't you forgotten something?" asked Sandy.

"Sure!" shouted Tommy. "I'm forgetting to eat!"

"And you're forgetting something else!" insisted Sandy.

"Nix on the forget!" declared Tommy. "When I forget my eatings and sleepings, the world will come to an end!"

"You forgot to read a chapter in your dream book!" said Sandy.

"Never you mind that dream book," Tommy replied. "Whenever you want to find the answer to any puzzle, you look in that dream book!"

After eating another hearty meal the boys, having already packed their wardrobes, locked the door of their room and addressed themselves to slumber.

They were awakened about five o'clock by a loud knocking on the door, and presently they heard the voice of Canfield calling to them.

V. T. Sherman

"Wake up, boys!" he cried. "I have good news for you!"

"All right, let her go!" shouted Tommy.

"The pumps are working, and the water is lowering in the mine!"

"That's nice!" laughed Sandy.

"And we've found out what caused the sudden flooding," the caretaker went on. "It seems that a partition, or wall, between the Labyrinth and the Mixer mines unaccountably gave way. The Mixer mine has been flooded for a long time and, as it lies above the level of the Labyrinth, the water naturally flowed into our mine as soon as the wall was down."

"But what caused the partition to fall?" asked Will, opening the door for the admission of the caretaker.

"No one knows!" was the answer.

"If you look about a little," Tommy suggested, "I think you'll find traces of dynamite. Who discovered the break in the dividing wall?"

"A gang under the leadership of Ventner, the detective!" was the reply.

The caretaker was very much surprised and not a little annoyed at the effect his answer had upon the four boys.

"I don't see anything humorous about that!" he said as the lads threw themselves down on the bunks and roared with laughter.

"It looks funny to me!" Tommy replied. "If we had never

showed up here, the mine wouldn't have been flooded. As soon as we start away or promise to leave the district, which amounts to the same thing, this cheap skate of a detective finds the break, and all is well again!"

"Why, you don't think that he had anything to do with the trouble at the mine, do you?" questioned the caretaker.

"Oh, of course not!" replied Sandy. "Ventner had nothing to do with cutting the ladder! That fellow will land in state's prison if he keeps on trying to murder boys by sawing ladder rungs!"

"I had forgotten that," said Canfield.

"Well, don't forget that this man Ventner is playing the chief villain's role in this drama!" Tommy advised. "And another thing you mustn't forget," the boy continued, "is that you're not to say a word to him that will inform him that he is suspected."

"I think I can remember that!" replied the caretaker.

The boys prepared a hasty supper and then, suit cases in hand, started for the little railway station. There they inquired about the arrival and departure of trains, bought tickets, and made themselves as conspicuous as possible about the depot.

"Keep your eye out for the third boy," George chuckled, as the lads walked up and down the platform.

"Don't get excited about the third boy," Will replied. "We'll find him when the right time comes!"

"There's Ventner!" exclaimed Tommy as the detective came

rushing down the platform. "Of course the good, kind gentleman would want to bid us farewell!"

"I'd like to crack him over the coco!" exclaimed Sandy.

"I'll bet he's got some kind of a fake story to tell," suggested Will. "He looks like a man who had been working his imagination overtime!"

"News of the two boys!" shouted the detective as he came up smiling.

CHAPTER X

THE BOY IN THE "EMPTY"

"Didn't I tell you," whispered Will, "that he is there with a product of his imagination? If you leave it to him, the two boys we're in search of are somewhere on the Pacific slope!"

"He must think we're a lot of suckers to take in any story he'll tell!" whispered Tommy. "A person that couldn't get next to his game ought to be locked Up in the foolish house!"

"I've just heard from a railway brakeman," Ventner said, rushing up to the boys with an air of importance, "that the two lads you are in search of were seen leaving a box car at a little station in Ohio. I don't just recall the name of the station now, but I can find it by looking on the map! It seems the lads left here on the night following their departure from the breaker, and stole their passage to this little town I'm telling you about."

"Good thing you came to the depot," declared Will. "We should have been out of town in ten minutes more!"

"Where is this town?" asked George, thinking it best to show great interest in the statement made by the detective.

V. T. Sherman

"It's a little place on the Lake Erie & Western road!" was the answer.

The detective took a railroad folder from his pocket and consulted a map. It seemed to take him a long time to decide upon a place, but he finally spread the map out against the wall of the station and laid his finger on a point on the Lake Erie & Western railroad.

"Nankin is the name of the place. Strange I should have forgotten the name of the place. They were put out of the car at Nankin, and are believed to have started down the railroad right of way on foot."

"But you said they were seen leaving the car at Nankin!" Tommy cut in. "Now you say they were put out of the car!"

"Well, they were chased out of the car, and that covers both statements," replied the detective somewhat nervously.

"Thank you very much for the information!" Will exclaimed as the train the boys were to take came rolling into the station. "The pointer is undoubtedly a good one, and we'll take a look at the country about Nankin."

There was a crossing not more than six miles from the station where the boys had taken the train, and they were all ready to jump when the engineer slowed down and whistled his note of warning. It was quite dark, although stars were showing in a sky plentifully scattered over with clouds and, as the boys dropped down out of the illumination of the windows as soon as they struck the ground, they were not seen to leave the train by any of the passengers.

In a moment the train rushed on, leaving the four standing on the roadbed looking disconsolately in the direction of the town.

"Now for a good long hike!" exclaimed Tommy.

"It's for your own good!" laughed Sandy.

"I can always tell when anything's for my own good," Tommy contended.

"You don't look it!" chuckled Sandy.

"When anything's for my own good," the boy continued, "it's always disagreeable! It makes me think of a story I read once where the man complained that everything he ever wanted in this world was either expensive, indigestible or immoral."

"Well, get on the hike!" laughed George. "You can stand here and moralize till the cows come home, and it won't move you half an inch in the direction of the mine!"

"And look here," Will exclaimed as the boys started up the grade, "when we get within sight of the lights of the station, we must scatter and keep our traps closed! We can all make for the mine by different routes. Ventner thinks we are out of town now, and the chances are that he'll be plugging around trying to accomplish some purpose known only to himself. For my part I don't believe he is employed on the same case we are! He's working here for some outside parties!"

"That's the way it strikes me!" George agreed. "If the detective had been honestly trying to assist us, the mine wouldn't have been flooded, the pumps wouldn't have broken down, and the electric motors would have been found in excellent working order."

"Did you notice the suit he had on when he stood talking

V. T. Sherman

with us at the station?" asked Will. "That was a blue serge suit, wasn't it?"

"It surely was!" Tommy declared, quick to catch the point. "And there was a tear down the front of it which looked as if it had been made by the scraping of a saw! I guess if you'll match the shreds we found on the saw with the breaks in that coat front you'll find where the saw got in its work, all right!"

"And there was a cut on his hand, too!" Sandy observed. "Looked like he had bounced the saw off one of the rungs on top of a finger."

"Oh, he's a clever little boy all right!" Tommy cut in. "But he forgot to leave his brass band at home when he went out to cut into that ladder! If he does all his work the way he did that job, he'll be sitting in some nice, quiet state's prison before he's six months older."

When the boys came within a quarter of a mile of the station lights, they parted, Will and George turning off from the right of way and Sandy and Tommy keeping on for half a dozen rods. When the four boys were finally clear of the tracks they were walking perhaps twenty rods apart, and at right angles with the right of way.

"Now, as we approach the mine," Will cautioned his companion, "keep your eye out for Ventner and this third boy. They are both likely to be chasing around in the darkness."

The route to the mine taken by Tommy and his chum crossed a network of tracks, led up to the weigh-house and so on into the breaker. As they came to a line of empty cars standing on a spur they heard a movement in one of the empties and crouched down to listen.

"There's some one in there!" declared Tommy.

"Some old bum, probably!"

This from Sandy who had recently bumped his shins on a pile of ties and was not in a very pleasant humor.

"It may be the boy we're looking for!" urged Tommy.

Sandy sat down on the end of a tie and rubbed his bruised shin vigorously, muttering and protesting against railroad yards in general and this one in particular as he did so.

Tommy made his way under the empty and sat listening, his ear almost against the bottom of the car. Presently he heard a movement above and then it seemed to him that something of considerable weight was being dragged across the floor. This was followed in a moment by a slight groan, and then a shadowy figure leaped from the open side door and started away in the darkness.

Now Sandy had been warned to hang onto the third boy like grim death if he caught sight of him. He saw this figure bounce out of the car and start away. Therefore, he promptly reached out a foot and tripped the unknown to the ground.

He fell with a grunt of anger and pain and lay rolling on the cinders which lined the roadbed for a moment without speaking. In the meantime, Tommy had crawled out from under the car and stood ready to seize any second person who might make his appearance.

Almost immediately a second body came bouncing out of the empty.

Instead of starting away on a run, however, the second person stopped where Sandy stood beside the wiggling figure and looked down upon it.

"Hand him one!" he said in a boy's voice.

"Who is it?" asked Sandy.

"Don't know!" was the reply.

"What was he doing to you?"

"He was trying to rob me!"

"I don't think a man would get rich robbing people who ride in empties!" laughed Sandy. "I shouldn't think their bank rolls would make much of a hit with a bold, bad highwayman!"

"There's men riding the rods," was the reply, "who would kill a boy for a dime! If I wasn't opposed to cruelty to animals, I'd give this fellow a beating up right now. He tried to drag me from the car by the leg and nearly broke my ankle!"

"I heard him dragging you across the floor!" Tommy said, coming up to where the two boys stood. "Can you see who it is?" he added.

"He's just a tramp!" the other replied. "I saw him sneaking around the empties just before dark."

"Why were you sleeping in an empty?" asked Sandy.

"Because I like plenty of fresh air!" replied the boy with a chuckle.

While the boys talked the tramp arose and sneaked away,

limping over the ties as if tickled to death to get out of the way of the three youngsters.

As he disappeared in the darkness Tommy turned to the boy who had dropped out of the car to ask him a question.

The boy was nowhere to be seen.

"Now we've gone and done it!" cried Sandy.

"I guess we have!" agreed Tommy. "We've let the third boy get away from us! And we couldn't have done a worse thing!" he went on, "because the boys in the mine will know that we are still in this vicinity!"

While the boys stood blaming themselves the sharp call of the Wolf pack came to them.

V. T. Sherman

CHAPTER XI

A KNOCK AT THE DOOR

When Will and George came to the back of the weigh-house they heard some one moving about at the front.

"That's probably the caretaker, taking his last look for the night," suggested Will. "He pokes around all the outbuildings every night before he goes to bed. At least, he is supposed to."

"But this fellow hasn't got any lantern," urged George.

"The plot deepens!" chuckled Will.

"Can you crawl around there and see who it is," asked George, "or shall I go? It may be a thief, or it may be Ventner, or it may be this boy we're looking for. Anyway, we want to know who it is!"

"I'll go!" Will suggested, "and don't you make any racket if you hear something doing there. The one thing to do at this time is to keep our presence here a profound secret."

Will moved cautiously around the angle of the weigh-house just in time to see a figure leaving the side of the building and moving toward the breaker. There was a little side door in the breaker not far from the weigh-house, and it was toward this that the prowler was making his way.

Half way to the little house the fellow stumbled over some obstruction in his path and fell sprawling to the ground. He arose with an impatient oath and moved on again, but not before the watcher had recognized both the figure and the voice. Will turned back to where George stood.

"That's Ventner," he said.

"Are you sure?"

"Dead sure!"

There was a short silence.

"What can we do now?"

"I don't know of anything we can do, unless it is to watch the rascal and see where he goes," answered the other. "The chances are that he's trying to get into the mine!"

"That shows that the fellow's a crook," Will contended. "He has full permission to enter the mine at any time he sees fit."

"Of course, he's a crook!" agreed George. "What would he be sneaking around here in the night for, if he wasn't engaged in some underhand game? You just wait until we get into the mine," the boy continued, "and we'll give him a ghost scare that'll hold him for a while."

As Ventner approached the little side door leading into the breaker, a light flashed in the window of the room which the boys had occupied, and directly Canfield's voice was heard asking:

V. T. Sherman

"Who's there?"

"Now if he's on the square, hell answer!" whispered Will.

There was no reply whatever, and in a moment the caretaker called again, this time rather peremptorily:

"What are you prowling about the yard for?"

The detective dropped to his knees and began crawling away.

"If I see you around here again," the caretaker shouted in a braver tone now that the intruder was taking his departure, "I'll do some shooting!"

Evidently giving over the attempt to enter the mine at that time, the detective arose to his feet as soon as he gained the shelter of the weigh-house, and walked away, passing as he did so, within a few feet of where the boys were standing.

"That settles that bum detective, so far as we are concerned!" Will said to his chum, in a whisper. "We knew before that he was playing a rotten game on us, but we didn't know that his plans included such surreptitious visits to the mine."

After making sure that the detective was not within sight or sound, Will and George tapped softly at the little door and were admitted by the caretaker. Five minutes later they were joined by Tommy and Sandy.

"Were you boys out there a few moments ago?" asked Canfield.

"Nix!" replied George. "That was Ventner. We saw him from the weigh-house. He was trying to sneak his way into the mine!"

"But he has full permission to enter at any time he sees fit!" urged the caretaker. "It doesn't seem as if he would attempt to steal his way in during the night. You must be mistaken!"

"Yes, and perhaps we were mistaken about the sawing of the ladder, too!" Tommy broke in.

"Yes, we may all be mistaken about that."

"Not so you could notice it!" declared Sandy. "If you look at the thief's coat, you'll see that he didn't do all the sawing on the rungs of the ladder. We've got him too dead to skin!"

Without any lights being shown on the surface, the boys were conducted down the ladder to the first level. There they found a room very cosily furnished, indeed. A lounge from the office, a couple of good sized cupboards, and a large table had been brought down, together with a serviceable rug and numerous chairs, and the apartment presented an unexpectedly homelike appearance.

The current was on, and two electric lamps made the room as light as day. The cooking was to be done over electric coils so that the presence of the boys would not be disclosed by smoke. One of the ventilating pipes which supplied the offices in the vicinity of the shaft with fresh air passed through the room, so there was no lack of ozone.

"Have we got plenty of eatings?" asked Tommy.

"Plenty!" was the reply. "I have arranged for fresh meat, milk and vegetables to be brought in every evening."

"Talk about your bull-headed, obstinate men!" exclaimed

Tommy, as the caretaker finally took his departure. "That fellow takes the cake! He knows very well that we caught Ventner in the act of sawing on the ladder, and he knows, too, that we heard Wolf calls while we were in the mine. Still, he shakes his head and says that he don't know about the boys being there, and don't know about that bum detective being crooked. If you could get a saw and operate on his head, you'd find it solid bone!"

"You'll feel better after you get supper!" Sandy declared.

"This isn't any grouch!" insisted Tommy. "This is the true story of that man's life! If I had a dollar for every time he doesn't know anything, I'd be the richest boy in the world!"

"Are you thinking of going down the mine tonight?" asked George, with a wink at Will. "We might try another midnight excursion."

"If you kids go into the mine tonight," declared Will, "I'll send you both back to Chicago on the first train!"

"Aw, how are you going to find these boys if you don't go into the mine?" demanded Tommy. "I suppose you'll want us to wait till daylight when the owners will be looking around to see if any damage was done by the inundation. The best time is at night!"

"Look here," Will argued, "we've got to do more than lay hands on the boys! We've got to find out why they are hiding in the mine."

"That's the correct word," agreed George. "Hiding is the word that expresses the situation exactly!"

"There is no doubt," Will continued, "that the boys were sent here by some one for some specific purpose. They are hiding in the mine with a well-defined motive. I have an idea that we might be able to find them in twenty-four hours, but what is more important, is to find out what they are up to."

"Well, in order to get the whole story, we'll have to pretend that we are looking for them and can't find them!" George said.

"That's right!" laughed Tommy. "Give them plenty of rope and they'll hang themselves. We may as well have the whole story while we're at it."

Before preparing their beds for the night, the boys paid a visit to the shaft and made their way down to the rungs which had been cut. They found that they had been replaced by new ones.

There was still water in the lower levels of the mine, but it was slowly disappearing through the sump, and the indications were that it would be dry by morning. The boys listened intently for some evidence of occupancy as they moved up and down the shaft, but all was still.

"This would be a good place to tell a ghost story," Tommy chuckled as they moved back to their room on the first level.

"There's about a million stories now, entitled The Ghost of the Mine!" declared Sandy. "Perhaps however," he went on, "one more wouldn't hurt."

"If I see a ghost tonight," declared Tommy, "it'll be in my dreams!"

Sandy and Tommy were sound asleep on their cots as soon as supper was over, and Will and George were getting ready to retire when the soft patter of a light footstep sounded in the vicinity of the shaft.

"Rats must be thick in the mine!" suggested George.

"Rats nothing!" declared Will. "Those two youngsters are prowling about in order to see what we are up to!"

As he spoke the boy arose, turned off the electric light and stepped out into the passage.

CHAPTER XII

A MIDNIGHT ROBBER

There was a quick scamper of feet as Will stepped out, then silence!

"Where did he go?" asked George, joining his chum on the outside.

"Down the ladder!" replied Will.

"Why don't we go and see where he went?"

"That might be a good idea," Will replied. "Do you think it's safe for us to try to navigate that shaft in the dark?"

"We can stick to the ladders, can't we?" asked George.

"We ought to find out where the kids hang out," Will argued. "I'd like to get my hands on one of them!"

"I don't think we're likely to do that tonight," George answered. "It seems to me that about the only way we can catch those fellows is to set a bear trap. They seem to be rather slippery."

V. T. Sherman

Will, clad only in pajamas and slippers, moved toward the shaft, and looked down. It was dark and still below, and he turned back with a little shudder. The situation was not at all to his liking.

"Well, are you going down?" asked George.

"Sure, I'm going down!" Will answered. "I'm only waiting to get up my nerve! It looks pretty dreary down there. If we could use a light I wouldn't mind, but it's pretty creepy going down that hole in the darkness."

"Then suppose we wait until morning," suggested George.

Will leaned against the shaft timbers and laughed.

"It'll be just as dark in here in the morning, as it is now!" he said. "I think we'd better go on down tonight and see if we can locate the fellows."

The two boys passed swiftly down the ladder, paused a moment at the second level, and then passed on to the third. The gangways leading out from the shaft were reasonably dry now. Lower down the dip they were still under a few inches of water.

"I don't see how we're going to discover anybody down in this blooming old well!" George grumbled. "There might be a regiment of state troops here and we wouldn't be able to see a single soldier!"

"We can't show a light, for all that!" declared Will. "We've just got to wait and see if *they* won't be kind enough to show a light."

"You guessed it," chuckled George, whispering softly in his

chum's ear, "there's a glimmer of light, now!"

"I see it!" Will replied.

The boys left the ladder and moved out into the center gangway. They could see a light flickering some distance in advance, and had no difficulty in following it.

"That's an electric torch!" Will commented.

"Perhaps, if we follow along, we'll be able to track them to their nest," George suggested, "and, still, I don't care about getting very far away from the shaft. We might get lost in these crooked passages."

"Yes," replied Will. "Some one might head us off, too. I don't care about being held up here in pajamas."

The mine was damp and cold, and a wind was sweeping up the passage toward the shaft. The boys shivered as they walked, yet kept resolutely on until the light they were following left the main gangway and disappeared in a cross heading.

"That means 'Good-night' for me," whispered Will, "for I'm not going to get out beyond the reach of the rails. I guess well have to go back and invent some other means of trapping those foxy boys."

As Will spoke the light reappeared and moved on down the gangway again. Then, for the first time, the boys saw a figure outlined against the illumination. Will caught his chum by the arm excitedly.

"That isn't one of the boys at all!" he exclaimed.

"Well, how large a population do you think this mine has!" demanded George. "If it isn't one of the boys, who is it?"

"That bum detective!" answered Will.

"So he got in here at last, did he?" chuckled George. "Well, it's up to us to find out what he's doing in here!"

"Do you think that is the gink who was prowling around our room?" asked Will. "If he is, then our little trip in the country doesn't count for much!"

"The fellow who visited us," George argued, "was light and quick on his feet. This bum detective waddles along like an old cow."

"Then we've passed the boy who called to see us, and failed to leave a card," grinned Will. "We may meet him as we return!"

"Here's hoping we bump straight into him if we do meet him," George exclaimed. "I'm just aching to get my hands on that fellow!"

"I'm not particularly anxious to catch him just yet," Will suggested. "I want to find out what the kids are up to before we pounce down upon them."

While the boys stood in the passage, whispering together, the light moved on until it came to a chamber which seemed to be rather shallow, for the reflection of the searchlight was still in the gangway.

"Now we've got him!" exclaimed Will. "I think I remember that chamber, and, unless I'm very much mistaken, it opens only on this passage! While he's poking around in there, we'll sneak up and see what he's doing!"

Before the boys reached the entrance to the chamber they heard the sounds of a pick. When they came nearer and looked in they saw the detective poking away at a heap of "gob" which lay in one corner of the excavation. He worked industriously, and apparently without fear of discovery. Now and then he stooped down to peer into a crevice in the wall, but soon went on again.

"I wonder if he thinks he can find two boys in that heap of refuse?" laughed George. "I wonder why he don't use a microscope."

The detective busied himself at the heap of refuse for a considerable length of time, and then began a further investigation of little breaks in the wall. Using his pick to enlarge the openings he made a systematic search of one break after another.

"Looks like he might be hunting after some pirate treasure," George chuckled. "I never heard of Captain Kidd sailing over into the sloughs of Pennsylvania. Did you?"

"That tells the story!" Will whispered. "The fellow is here on some mission of his own. That story of his about being in quest of the boys is all a bluff! I reckon he had heard somewhere that two boys were missing and came here with the fairy tale!"

"Well, he's got a good, large mine to look in if he's in search of treasure," George suggested. "He can spend the rest of his days here, provided the operators don't get sore on him."

While the boys looked, Ventner turned toward the entrance to the chamber, and they scampered away. Turning back, they saw him pass out of the place where he had been working and into a similar excavation farther on. There he worked as industriously as before.

"You see how it is," Will suggested. "The fellow is hunting for something, and doesn't know where to look for it! So it's all right to let him go ahead with his quest for hidden wealth, or whatever it is he's after. When he finds it, we'll not be far away!"

"I like this walking about in my naked feet," George grunted in a moment. "I had my slippers on when I came down the ladder, but I either had to take them off and carry them in my hands or lose them in the mud."

"Same here!" Will said. "I'm going back to my little cot bed right now and go to sleep. I think we have the detective sized up and we can catch the kids some other night."

"Me for the hay, too," George exclaimed. "I don't think I was ever quite so sleepy in my life!"

"Now, on the way back," Will cautioned, "we ought to keep still and keep a sharp lookout for the person who was sneaking around our quarters."

"Whoever it was may be between us and the shaft," George suggested.

"If I thought so," Will argued, "I'd just stand around and wait until they pass us on the way in. I don't want to find those boys just now. There's a mystery connected with this mine which the caretaker knows nothing about, and which Mr. Horton never referred to when he sent us down here.

"We wouldn't be able to breathe if we didn't discover an air of mystery every fifteen minutes," George declared.

Half way back to the shaft, the boys, who were walking very softly in their stockinged feet, heard a rattle as of a moving stone or piece of coal in the passage, and at once drew up against the side wall.

While they stood there, scarcely daring to breathe, they sensed that some one was passing them in the darkness. The tread was light and brisk, and they thought they heard a soft chuckle as the unseen figure breezed by them.

"I'll bet the lad who was listening near our door never came down the shaft until after we did!" George whispered after the figure had passed by.

"That's very likely!" agreed Will.

"Then he may have been poking around our quarters while we have been gone."

"That's very likely, too."

Believing the way to be clear now, the boys hastened on toward the shaft. Just as they reached the foot of the ladder they heard a sound which sent the blood throbbing to their cheeks.

"He's making fun of us!" exclaimed George.

"It looks like it," admitted Will.

The sound they heard was the low, complaining snarl of the Wolf.

"The nerve of him!" exclaimed George.

V. T. Sherman

"Perhaps he'll answer now!" Will suggested.

Then followed the "slap, slap, slap!" of the Beaver Patrol.

No answer came from the darkness beyond the shaft.

"He's got his nerve with him!" declared Will. "When I get hold of him, I'll teach him to answer Boy Scout challenges!"

When the boys got back to their quarters they found Tommy and Sandy sitting in the darkness with their automatics and their searchlights in their hands. One of them turned on a finger of light as the boys entered but immediately shut it off again.

"What's coming off here?" demanded Will.

"Do you know what those fellows did?" asked Tommy. "They came here while we were asleep and stole about half our provisions!"

CHAPTER XIII

ONE MORE HUNGRY BOY

"We may as well turn on the lights!" Will said. "If any one comes in here to steal Tommy's necktie," he added with a wink at his chum, "we want to see what he looks like."

"Why didn't you stay here and watch, then?" demanded Tommy. "Why did you go off and leave the camp all alone? I heard people moving around, and I thought it was you."

Will and George sat down on the edge of their cots and laughed.

"Yes, you thought it was me!" Will said directly. "You never heard a thing! You'd better look and see if the midnight visitors didn't steal your pajamas. Or they might have taken your pillow."

Tommy threw a shoe at his tormentor and turned on the electric light.

"Now that I'm awake," he said with a sly grin, "I think that I'll get myself something to eat. Seems to me I'm always hungry."

V. T. Sherman

While the boy rattled among canned goods and candled eggs to see if they were fit for a four-minute boil, Sandy turned to George.

"What did you find in the mine?" he asked.

"We found that bum detective nosing around. We've got his number now, all right," the boy went on, "and there's something in the mine that he wants to find and he doesn't know where to look for it. He isn't looking for Jimmie and Dick any more than we're looking for a pot of gold at the end of a rainbow. I don't believe he was ever sent here to make a search for the missing boys!"

"What was he doing when you saw him?" asked Sandy.

"Poking around in worked-out chambers with a pick!"

"Did he see you?"

"You bet he didn't! Do you think we're going to walk six miles in from the country in order to dodge the detective, and then let him run across us in the mine?"

"Yes, but what's he looking for?" insisted Sandy.

"That, me son," George replied with a wink, "is locked in the bosom of the future! We may be able to find out what he's doing here when we find out who struck Billy Patterson."

"Don't get gay now!" grinned Sandy.

"Well, if you insist upon it," George continued with a smile, "Ventner was digging in refuse heaps for something which he didn't find!"

"Did you meet the boys who stole our provisions?" was the next question. "I wish you'd got hold of them!"

"We are certain that one of them passed us while we were returning," George answered.

"The nerve of him!" shouted Sandy.

"The idea of his coming here and swiping our provisions!" Tommy cut in. "If I ever get hold of that gink, I'll beat his head off!"

"You going back after than bum detective tonight?" asked George.

"Not me!" answered Sandy. "Me for ham and eggs!"

"What's the matter with passing the ham and eggs around?"

Every one of the four boys sprang forward as the words came from somewhere just outside the door.

"That's one of those thieving kids!" declared Tommy.

"You've had your share!" shouted Sandy.

"It has now been nine days since I've tasted food!" came the answer from the other side of the door, and the boys thought they caught a chuckle between the words.

"All right!" replied Tommy. "You go and sit in the deserted mine nine days more, and then we'll consider whether you have any right to be hungry. Go on away tonight, anyhow!"

"Not so you could notice it," came the insistent tones from beyond the door. "I'm going to stay right here until I get something to eat!"

"Eat the stuff you stole!" advised Sandy.

"You're in wrong!" came from the other side of the door. "I haven't had a thing to eat in forty or fifty days. Come on, now," he added "be good fellows and open up. I'm so hungry I could eat a brass cylinder."

"Aw, let him in!" advised Tommy. "He'll stand there chinning all night if we don't! We've got enough to eat for the present anyway."

Will unfastened the door and a tall, slender young fellow of perhaps seventeen stepped inside the room and stood blinking a moment under the strong electric light. His face was streaked with coal dust and his clothing was ragged and dirty. Still, the boy looked like anything but a tramp. Tommy eyed him suspiciously for a moment.

"Where'd you come from?" he asked.

"Off the rods!" was the reply.

"And I suppose," Sandy broke in, "that you were just taking a stroll by starlight and just happened to walk into this mine."

"Sure!" answered the other with a provoking grin.

"Well, if anybody should ask you," Tommy continued, "you're the boy that had a mixup with the tramp tonight, and ran away while we were trying to invite you to supper. What do you know about that?"

"Invite me to supper now and see if I'll run away!"

"If you boys will cut out this foolish conversation for a minute," Will suggested, "I'll try to find out what this boy wants. Do you mean to say," he added turning to Tommy, "that you bumped into this kid while returning to the mine from the tracks?"

"Didn't I tell you about that?" asked Tommy. "I thought I did. We found him in a mixup with a tramp, and that's all there is to it!"

"And I told you at the time," the stranger interrupted, "that the tramp tried to rob me! That was all right, too. He did try to rob me, but I didn't have a blessed cent in my possession, so he didn't get anything! The tramp who got a hold of me night before last stripped me clean! And that, you see, is why I haven't got any money to buy provisions with. And also that's the reason why I'm hungry."

The four boys gathered around the stranger and began a systematic course of questions which at first brought forth only unsatisfactory answers.

"And also," the boy went on, taking up the speech he had begun some minutes before, "that's why two other boys are hungry just about this time. I got rolled for my wad plenty."

"That's South Clark street!" laughed Tommy.

"That's Bowery!" corrected the other.

"What'd you say about other boys being hungry?" asked Sandy.

"I said that's why two other boys are hungry."

"They ain't hungry any more," Tommy declared with a wink.

"That listens good!" the stranger said.

"Because," continued Tommy, "they came in here about an hour ago and stole everything they could get their hands on."

"Brave boys!" laughed the other.

"You wasn't hiding behind the door when they gave out nerve, either!" declared Tommy. "Here these boys come here and steal our grub and you seem to think they did a noble thing! What's your name, anyhow?"

"Buck," was the reply. "Elmer Cyrus Buck, 409 Lexington Avenue, N. Y. C. Member of the Wolf Patrol, Boy Scouts of America, and just about ready to scrap for something to eat!"

"Why didn't you say so before?" Tommy exclaimed, setting a great slice of ham and several freshly boiled eggs, together with bread and butter and canned tomatoes, before the young man. "Why didn't you say something about being a Boy Scout before you tried to hold us up for a hand-out? You seem to go at everything wrong end first!"

"How long since you've seen Jimmie Maynard and Dick Thompson?" asked Will. "You must have failed to connect with them tonight!"

"How do you know that?"

"Because, if you had bumped into them, they would have fed you out of the provisions they stole from us!"

"I haven't been looking for them tonight!" Elmer replied. "I tried to follow you to the mine," he added turning to Tommy and Sandy, "when you left me at the car. But, somehow, I lost track of you in the darkness, and when you finally got into the mine, I had to wait for things to quiet down before I could force an entrance. I don't think I could have got in at all if some one hadn't been ahead of me with a jimmy, or an axe, or something of that kind."

"That must have been Ventner," suggested Will.

"Mother of Moses!" cried Elmer. "Has that fellow got into the mine again? Does he know you're here?"

"He knew that we were here," was the answer, "but he thinks we've gone away! He's down in the mine now, hunting for a pot of diamonds in the refuse cast aside by the miners."

"Well you got into the mine at last," Will suggested, "what is the next move you are thinking of making?"

"After I finish my modest supper," Elmer answered, with a nod at the great stack of food which Tommy had piled up on his plate, "I'm going to give you boys the surprise of your lives!"

"You've pretty near done that now!" laughed Will.

"And I'm going to begin," Elmer resumed, "by fishing two members of the Wolf Patrol out of the mine and bringing them up here to apologize for stealing your grub!"

"If you'll do that," replied Will, "we'll forgive you!"

CHAPTER XIV

MINE RATS READY FOR WAR

"Wait till I destroy this hen fruit," Elmer said, "and I'll go down and bring those two foolish youngsters up with me. It's time we had an understanding with you boys. You're here looking for something, and we're here looking for something. Perhaps we would meet with better success if we talked over our plans."

"What are you looking for?" demanded Tommy.

"Keep it dark," grinned Elmer. "I'm not going to tell you a thing until I bring Jimmie and Dick up here so they can get next to the whole story! I guess you boys can work together without scrapping, can't you?"

"When we find the boys," laughed Will, "our job will come to an end!"

"So that's what you came down here after, is it?"

"Yes, we came here to dig two boys out of a mine."

"I don't believe it!" replied Elmer.

"We came here from Chicago for that very purpose," went on Will.

"Who sent you here?" asked Elmer.

"Lawyer Horton."

"Then Lawyer Horton didn't tell you the whole story," laughed Elmer. "He held out on you boys, just to see if you wouldn't get the story at the mine. Of course he didn't know where we were at the time he sent you down here, but he never sent you for the express purpose of finding us!"

"Then why did he send us?" asked Tommy.

"You just wait till I go and bring up Jimmie and Dick, and I'll tell you all about it! I won't be gone more than a minute."

"But hold on!" cried Sandy. "You mustn't go chasing down into the mine now. That bum detective is there, and we don't want him to know that we're anywhere within a hundred miles of this place."

"He doesn't know that we're here, either," commented Elmer. "His notion is that he drove us all into the next state when he caused the mine to be flooded. He thinks he has the whole mine to himself now."

"So he caused the mine to be flooded, did he?"

"Sure he did," was the curt reply. "The boys saw him digging away at the wall which protects this dry mine from the wet one next door."

"So you saw him doing it, did you?"

"I didn't, because I haven't been in the mine before for any length of time, but Jimmie and Dick saw him."

"We've been told that he made the trouble," Will agreed, "but we weren't so very sure of it, after all. At least, we didn't have the proof. He ought to get twenty years for that!"

"Well, if you keep asking me questions all night," Elmer declared, "I'll never get the boys up here, and you'll never know why you were sent here! You can come along with me if you want to."

"But how about this detective?" insisted Sandy.

"We ought to be able to get the boys up here without letting him know that we are in the mine," answered Elmer. "We needn't travel with a fife and drum corps ahead of us, nor even carry any lights down with us. He's probably working in some inside chamber."

"All right," Will answered, "we've had our trip through the mine tonight, so we'll let Tommy and Sandy go with you. Are you sure the boys will come if you ask them to?"

"Sure they'll come!" was the reply.

The two boys drew on their rubber boots with which they had provided themselves before taking up their quarters in the mine, and which they had been too excited to use on a previous occasion, and Will loaned a pair to Elmer, then they started down the ladders.

"It would be something of a joke if we should butt into that detective now, wouldn't it?" Sandy laughed, as they passed down from the second level.

"I shouldn't consider it much of a joke," replied Tommy. "We took a lot of pains to make him think we'd gone out of town!"

As the boys walked softly down the center gangway they heard a fall of rock which seemed to come from the passage next north. This passageway was connected by the main one with a cross-heading situated perhaps three hundred feet from the shaft.

"I don't know much about mines," whispered Elmer as the boys stopped and listened to the clatter of the rocks as they settled down on the floor of the cavern, "but that sounds to me a whole lot like a fall from the roof. I hope the boys are not injured."

The boys walked faster until they came to the cross-passage and then turned to the right. Just as they left the main gangway, they heard the sound of running feet and directly the distant creaking of the ladder rungs.

"Some one's making a hot-foot for the surface!" exclaimed Tommy.

"That's Ventner!" declared Sandy.

"How do you know that?"

"Because he wears heavy boots. We have rubbers on, and Jimmie and Dick, who are down in the mine, are also wearing rubber boots!"

"The farther he gets away from the mine, the better it will suit me," Elmer broke in. "I wish he'd go away and stay for a hundred years!"

"The chances are that he dug away one of the pillars and caused that drop from the roof," suggested Sandy.

"I guess that's all right, too," Elmer argued. "If he's been digging around here the way the boys say he has, he's certainly taking chances on cutting down more than one column. He ought to be fired out of the mine!"

The boys now came to a chamber across the entrance to which a great mass of shale had been thrown when the fall from the roof took place.

At first they listened, fearful that they would hear the voices of the lads they were in search of beyond the wall, possibly crushed under the weight of the mass of stone. Then they passed along for a short distance and peered into the chamber over the heap of refuse.

What they saw brought excited exclamations to their lips.

Jimmie and Dick stood in the interior of the chamber, hedged in by fallen debris. They were swinging their searchlights frantically from side to side, and while the boys looked, they began, the utterance of such yells as had never before been heard in that gloomy place.

"What's the trouble?" asked Elmer, showing his light at the narrow opening between the roof of the chamber and the pile of refuse.

"Oh, you're there, are you?" asked one of the boys. "We thought perhaps you'd gone back to New York and left us to starve to death."

"Well, you didn't starve, did you?" asked Elmer.

"Wow, wow, wow!" yelled Jimmie.

"Now, what is it?" asked Elmer.

"Rats!" yelled the boy. "Millions of rats! They're creeping out by the regiment from behind the cribbing where we were hidden!"

"That idiot of a detective," the other boy went on, "undermined a pillar and let about half an acre of roof down into this chamber. When the roof fell, it broke the cribbing and the rats began pouring out."

"They won't hurt you!" declared Tommy. "Only you mustn't go to picking a quarrel with them. They're fighters when they get their tempers up. Just let them alone and they'll let you alone!"

"Who's that talking?" demanded Jimmie.

"That's the relief expedition!" laughed Elmer.

"You ought to be fired out of the Wolf Patrol for not answering Boy Scout signals!" Tommy broke in. "We called to you more than a dozen times, and you never answered once!"

"Well, we had to wait until Elmer reported what kind of fellows you were, didn't we?" asked Dick. "We couldn't go and make friends with you without knowing what you were here for, so we kept out of your way until Elmer could find a way to learn more about you."

"And instead of finding a way," Jimmie took up the argument, "he goes off and gets lost in a thicket about six feet square and never shows up with any grub for twenty-four hours! So we had to go and steal grub off the boys!"

"Yes, and we're going to have you pinched when you get out!" laughed Tommy. "You'll get ninety days for that."

"Where'd that bum detective go?" asked Jimmie. "When the roof fell, we heard him go clattering down the gangway running as though he had only about thirty seconds in which to get to New York."

"He's a long distance from the mine by this time," Elmer suggested.

"Well," Jimmie said, "I don't like the company of these rats, so if you'll kindly dig into the refuse on your side, we'll work from this side and we'll soon be out. These rats look hostile."

"You let 'em alone!" advised Tommy.

"Yes, I'll let 'em alone—not!" shouted Jimmie. "You wait until I get an armful of rocks and I'll beat some of their heads off!"

"For the love of Mike, don't do anything of the kind!" yelled Tommy. "They'll climb onto you nine feet thick if you injure one of them!"

But it was too late! Jimmie acquired an armful of large sized pieces of slate and began tossing them into the huddle of rats in the corner.

For an instant the rats squealed viciously as they Were struck by the sharp edges of the slate, then they seemed to confer together for a moment or two, then they spread out like a fan and began moving toward the two boys.

"Now you've done it!" cried Tommy. "If you don't get out of there in about a second, the rats'll eat your legs off!"

Without waiting for the boys to assume the offensive, the rats began screaming and springing at their feet.

The three boys on the outside of the barrier, understanding the peril their friends were in, crawled up to the top of the wall of refuse which shut the boys into the chamber and turned their lights inside.

It seemed to them then that the rats were two or three deep on the floor. There appeared to be hundreds—thousands of them. They circled around the boys, becoming bolder every moment. They nipped at the rubber boots and left the marks of their teeth on the tough uppers.

"Now, boys," Tommy yelled, as they drew their automatics and leveled them over the wall, "shoot to kill! This is no Sunday School picnic! And while we're shooting, boys, you back up to this wall, and see if you can't work your way to the top. If you can get up here, we can manage to displace enough slate to let you through."

The boys fired volley after volley, but the rats came on viciously.

CHAPTER XV

STICK OF DYNAMITE

By this time Jimmie and Dick had their automatics out and were firing into the horde of rats. They killed the rodents by the score, yet for every one slaughtered a dozen seemed to appear.

Presently the chamber became so full of powder smoke, the air so stifling, that the lads were obliged to cease firing.

"Work your way up this wall," Tommy cried out to the lads as he heard them panting below. "Work your way up so we can catch hold of you, and you'll soon be out of that mess!"

"There's a dozen rats hanging to my boots!" cried Dick.

"And mine, too!" declared Jimmie.

The three boys on the outside continued to hurl refuse from the top of the wall into the chamber. This in a measure kept the rats back, and before many minutes Jimmie and Dick were drawn to the top of the barrier.

Their rubber boots were cut in scores of places by the sharp teeth of the rats, and even their clothing as high up as their shoulders showed ragged tears. A dozen or more rats hung to the boys' boots until the top was reached, then they dropped back screaming with baffled rage.

"Talk about your wild Indians!" exclaimed Tommy. "I never saw anything as vicious as that was! I told you boys not to open up an argument with those fellows! Mine rats are noted for their courage when attacked."

"How many bites did you get?" asked Elmer anxiously.

"I got half a dozen nips!" answered Jimmie.

"And so did I," Dick cut in.

"Well, you boys ought to get back to the room right away," Tommy suggested, "and have peroxide applied to the wounds. I've known of people dying of blood poison occasioned by rat bites."

"Have you got it in camp with you?" asked Elmer.

"We're the original field hospital!" laughed Tommy. "We never leave Chicago without taking with us everything needed in the first aid to the wounded line. We'd be nice Boy Scouts to go poking about the country with nothing with which to heal our wounds!"

"Boys," Elmer now said, with a mischievous grin on his face, "I want to introduce you to Jimmie Maynard and Dick Thompson. I've heard that your names are Sandy and Tommy, but that's all I know about it!"

"Green and Gregory!" laughed Tommy. "My name's Gregory. Sandy's name isn't Sandy at all, but Charley. We call him Sandy because he looks like he'd been rolled in sand."

"Well, we may as well be getting back to headquarters!" declared Sandy after these original introductions had been made. "But hold on," he continued turning back to Jimmie and Dick, with a look on his face intended to be severe, "aren't you going to bring our provisions back?"

"The provisions," laughed Jimmie, "were hidden in the chamber where the rats were, and you're welcome to all you can get your hands on now!"

"Oh, well," Sandy groaned, "I suppose we'll have to buy more."

"One difficulty about passing in and out of the mine so frequently," Tommy stated, "is that this man Ventner is likely to catch us at it. There's no knowing what he'll do next if he finds that we're searching the place. According to Elmer, you know," he continued, "we didn't finish our job when we landed on you boys. He says the real game is now about to begin."

"He's right there!" declared Jimmie.

"Strange thing Mr. Horton didn't tell us all about it!" complained Tommy. "Where was the use of his sending us down here and making monkeys of us? He ought to be ashamed of himself!"

"He wanted to see whether you could find out what you were here for!" laughed Elmer. "Perhaps he understood that after you caught us, we'd tell you all about it. He's a pretty foxy guy, that man Horton, from all I hear about him! I'm going to Chicago some day to meet him!"

"Well, what is it we've got to look for now?" demanded Sandy.

"You just wait till we get to headquarters!" replied Jimmie.

"We ought to do that just as quickly as possible," Tommy ventured, "because there's no knowing when that bum detective may return. I'd give a whole lot of money right now to know what he is looking for!"

The three strangers regarded each other laughingly, evidently well pleased at the puzzled look showing on the faces of their friends.

"Wait till we get to headquarters and get a square meal under our belts," Jimmie promised, "and we'll tell you what this bum detective is looking for. It won't take long to do it, either."

"You know, then, do you?" asked Tommy.

"Of course, we know!"

"Then why don't you tell?"

"Couldn't think of telling on an empty stomach!" laughed Jimmie provokingly.

As the boys walked along the passage, only a short distance from the old tool house, they heard a rattling and bumping on the shaft ladders and instantly extinguished their lights.

Presently they heard footsteps on the hard floor of the gangway, and then a light such as those being used by the boys flashed out.

"Now we're in for it!" exclaimed Tommy.

"For the love of Mike, don't let him see us!" whispered Jimmie.

V. T. Sherman

"It'll spoil everything if he does," Dick submitted.

The boys crowded close against the wall of the gangway and waited impatiently for Ventner to pass along.

He was muttering to himself as he moved down the gangway, and his round, protruding belly and his little shapeless shoulders reminded the watching lads of the gnomes they had read about, living in underground cells and preying at night upon the fairies.

Only for a trifling accident the boys would certainly have been discovered. Just as the detective came to a position ten or fifteen feet from where they were standing, when he was in a position to see their faces by the rays cast on ahead by the flashlight, he partly turned his ankle in a stumble on the rails, and for a moment the rays of the light were directed downward. He hobbled along, raving and cursing, for a few steps and then walked briskly on again.

But the ever-watchful eye of the searchlight no longer struck upon the wall where the boys stood, and they realized that for the present they were safe from discovery. Ventner moved on down the gangway and soon disappeared in a cross cutting which ran to the right.

"That's lucky!" exclaimed Jimmie.

"Why didn't we geezle him?" demanded Tommy.

"Because we want his help!" replied Dick.

"His help?" laughed Sandy. "Yes, you'll get his help, all right! That fellow would get up in the middle of the night to do you a dirty trick, and don't you ever forget it!"

"That's the way he's going to help us!" laughed Elmer. "He'll get up in the middle of some dark night to do us a dirty trick, and before he knows what he's about, he'll be doing us a great kindness!"

"Suppose I slip back there and see what he's doing?" asked Tommy.

"Can you find your way back to headquarters alone?" asked Sandy.

"If I can't," asserted Tommy, "I won't be sending any wireless messages to you! If you think I'm likely to get lost, Dick can go back with me. He ought to know every corner in the old mine."

"Sure he does!" laughed Jimmie. "We've been travelling this mine for a good many nights now, and we know it like a book."

So Tommy and Dick started back down the passage, the intention being to hasten to the spot where Ventner had disappeared from the gangway, and then return to their companions immediately.

"We can't stay very long, you know," Tommy explained, "because you've got to have that peroxide dope put on your bites. It doesn't pay to fool with wounds of that description!"

"We'll be back to the old tool room as soon as they are!" answered Dick. "It will take only a minute to run down there and back!"

When the boys reached the cross-cutting into which Ventner had disappeared, they saw his light some distance away. It seemed to be in one of the chambers connected with the cross-cutting.

As they looked, the detective stepped forward into the circle of illumination and began working with a pick.

"Is he always doing that when you see him?" asked Tommy.

"You bet he is!" answered Dick.

"What's he doing it for?"

"You'll have to ask Elmer that."

"But you know, don't you?"

"Of course I know, but I'm not going to tell, because we all agreed that the story should never be told by any member of our party until Elmer got ready to tell it. So you see you've got to wait!"

"If I had my way about it," gritted Tommy, "I'd go back there and geezle that bum detective and wall him up in a chamber until he got hungry enough to tell the story himself. Then we wouldn't have to go sneaking around the mine in order to keep out of his way!"

"That would be a foolish move," insisted Dick, "because every stroke of the pick Ventner takes helps us along in the game we're playing."

"You're the original little mystery boy, ain't you?" said Tommy rather crossly. "All right, I'll get even."

The detective now moved farther along the cross-cutting and attacked a column of mingled rock and coal which helped to support the roof.

"The blithering idiot is going to try that trick again!" exclaimed Dick. "He'll have the whole mine down on our heads if he doesn't stop that business. He's always cutting down pillars."

"Just say the word," declared Tommy, "and I'll go stop him!"

"Let him go his own gait," replied Dick. "We'll manage to keep out of the way of the falls, and he can run his own chances."

Presently they saw the detective take something which resembled a stick of dynamite from a pocket and begin the work of setting it into the pillar. The boys moved hastily back.

"Now what do you think of that for a fool?" exclaimed Dick. "He'll have the whole mine down on our heads some day, just as sure as he's a foot high! I hope he'll be broken in two when the fall comes."

The boys stood some distance away watching the detective as he awkwardly manipulated the stick of dynamite.

V. T. Sherman

CHAPTER XVI

CAUSED BY A FALL

In the meantime Sandy, Elmer and Jimmie, reaching the old tool house, found Will and George very wide awake and doing the most extraordinary stunts of cooking.

"You said that your friends would be hungry," laughed Will, "and so we're preparing to feed them up fine. After that, you know, you've got to go on and tell us why we were sent down here without any real information as to the work we were to do."

"Where did you leave Tommy and Dick?" asked George.

"They went back to see what the detective was up to."

"So he's in the mine again, is he?"

"Yes," replied Sandy, "and if I had my way about it, he'd go out so quick that he'd think he'd struck a barrel of dynamite."

"If he keeps fooling with dynamite, he's likely to do that anyhow," Elmer cut in. "The boys say that he uses dynamite in the search of the mine he is making. He doesn't know how to use it, either!"

"Then he's got to be fired out of the mine!" declared Will. "We can't have him around here carrying dynamite in his clothes, and dropping it on the ground. You might as well give a baby a box of matches and a hammer to play with. Some day there'll be an explosion."

"Aw, leave him alone for a few days!" Jimmie advised. "He's doing us a lot of good just now, and we don't want to lose his help."

"His help?" repeated Will.

"He's bully help!" shouted George, with fine sarcasm.

"I guess I'll have to tell you about the mystery of the mine," Elmer laughed. "Tommy ought to be here to get the story with the rest, but you can tell him about it later on."

"He ought to be here any minute now," Jimmie asserted.

"Oh, he'll be here all right!" George argued. "Go on with the story. It's been hours since you came in here with the suggestion that there was a story, and you haven't told it yet!"

"Yes," Will interrupted, "get busy and tell us what Mr. Horton neglected to say when he sent us down here; and while you are about it," the boy went on, "you may as well tell us whether you really became lost in the mine, or whether you were sent here to do the very things you did do."

"Also," George broke in, "you may as well tell us what the detective is doing here, and how he is helping you in trying to blow up the mine."

"The boys were never lost in the mine a minute!" replied

Elmer, with a grin, "and Mr. Horton knew it. Mr. Horton received his instructions from Attorney Burlingame of New York, and I am positive that Burlingame gave his brother lawyer the whole story."

"Foxy game, eh?" laughed Will.

"I guess they wanted you to find out if we boys were of any account, and whether we were playing fair!" laughed Jimmie.

"Well, anyway, they expected you to find us and learn the story I'm now going to tell," Elmer continued.

"Je—rusalem!" exclaimed Will. "Why don't you get at it. That story has been jumping from tongue to tongue clothed in mystery for hours and we haven't been favored with it yet!"

"The story opens," Elmer began, "on a cold and stormy night in October in the year 1913. As the wind blew great gusts of rain down upon such pedestrians as happened to be out of doors—"

"Aw, cut it out!" exclaimed Will. "Why don't you go on and tell the story? We don't want any more of that Henry James business! You know he always has a solitary horseman proceeding slowly on foot."

"Well, it was a dark night, and a stormy one!" declared Elmer. "If it had been clear and bright, Stephen Carson, the Wall street banker, wouldn't have received a dent in his cupola. In stepping down from his automobile his foot slipped on the wet pavement, and he fell, striking on the back of his head."

"What's that got to do with this mine mystery?" demanded George.

"It has a great deal to do with this mine mystery," Elmer answered. "Stephen Carson arose from the ground, rubbed the back of his head with his gloved hand, and continued on his way to a meeting of a board of directors. He appeared to be perfectly sane and responsible for his acts at the meeting of the board, and when he left in his machine there were no indications that he had suffered more than a slight bruise from his fall. He was not seen at home again for two weeks."

"Now you begin to get interesting!" declared Will.

"Where did he go?" asked Sandy.

"That is what his friends don't know," replied Elmer.

"But he must have been seen somewhere!" insisted Sandy.

"He was!" answered Elmer. "He was seen in the vicinity of this mine!"

"Wow, wow, wow!" exclaimed Sandy.

"What was he doing here?" asked Will.

"Wandering about the premises."

"Now I can tell you the rest," Will said with a chuckle.

"Go on, then," advised Elmer.

"From the meeting of the board of directors that night," Will went on, whimsically, "this man Stephen Carson went directly to a safety deposit vault where three or four hundred thousand dollars' in the way of cash and jewelry, were hidden. He took the whole bundle and disappeared. Is that anywhere near right, Elmer?"

"Go on!" Elmer replied.

"Then in two weeks time he comes back and says that he don't know where he put the jewelry, but that he thinks he hid it in this mine. And, as they can't find any place where he hocked the jewelry, or put it up to carry out some gigantic Wall street plan, they are forced to believe that he really did mislay the jewelry while temporarily out of his head. Is that anywhere near right?"

"If you'll amend your report so as to show that he went to the Night and Day bank and drew out something over two hundred thousand dollars which he had on deposit there, and disappeared with the entire sum, you'll come nearer to the truth."

Will gave a long whistle of amazement.

"Two hundred thousand dollars in real money!" exclaimed George.

"Yes, he took two hundred thousand dollars in real money away with him that night," Elmer went on, "and when he returned to his home again, he was penniless and in rags."

"Was he in his right mind?" asked Will.

"He seemed to be."

"Has he now recovered from the injury he received that night?"

"So the doctors say."

"Then why doesn't he tell what he did with the money?"

"That part of his life is blank. He was seen in the vicinity of this mine, yet denies it. He was seen loitering in the woods not far away, but insists that he never visited this mine except to attend meetings of the board of directors."

"Now I've got you!" laughed Will. "His friends think he hid the money in this mine and we've been sent here to find it!"

"That's the idea," agreed Elmer.

"And this bum detective is here for the same purpose!"

"Yes, though where he received his information is more than I know. Upon his return to his home, Mr. Carson immediately made good the two hundred thousand dollars taken from the Night and Day bank and employed detectives to look up the missing coin.

"Is Ventner one of them?" asked Will.

"I don't think so," replied Elmer. "We were sent here to look through the mine, with the understanding that you were to come on from Chicago in a few days. Mr. Horton recommended you to Mr. Burlingame and so you were employed."

"Then this detective has no right here at all?"

"None whatever, so far as I can make out."

"Then why not fire him?"

"Because he may accidentally run across the money

V. T. Sherman

some day."

"If he does, he'll get away with it!" declared George.

"No, he won't," answered Elmer, "He'll be watched every minute from now on. You may be sure of that!"

"But you didn't seem to know what he was doing tonight," laughed Will.

"But I knew enough to come to the right place for the information I desired," replied Elmer.

"Strange thing Tommy and Dick don't come!" Sandy exclaimed, stepping to the door of the old tool house and listening intently. "They should have been here a long time ago!"

"Perhaps they've butted into Ventner," suggested Jimmie.

"They wouldn't do that," Elmer replied. "Every blow he strikes with his pick saves us the trouble of making one."

"You don't think he had any directions from anyone, do you?" asked Will. "You don't, think he knows where to look for the money any more than you do?"

"No, I think he just heard of the loss of the money and came down here on his own account."

"Well, if he's using dynamite in the mine," Will continued, "he ought to be turned out of it. If Mr. Carson really hid two hundred thousand dollars in currency in here, it's in some little pocket easy to find if we get into the right chamber. The use of dynamite might bury it twenty feet deep under a load of shale that would never be removed!"

"That's a fact!" cried Elmer.

The boys now stepped to the door and listened again, attracted by the sound of running feet.

"There's something doing!" exclaimed Sandy. "When Tommy comes home on a run, there's always something going on."

Directly the boys came panting up, stopping in the doorway to look behind them. They were both well winded.

"That bum detective back there," Tommy exclaimed, as soon as he could catch his breath, "is putting in dynamite enough to blow up the whole mine. He's attaching a long fuse, so he can get out before the explosion comes. We cried to get down far enough to choke off the fuse, but couldn't do it. In just about another minute, you'll hear something like a Fourth of July celebration!"

　　　　　　　V. T. Sherman

CHAPTER XVII

THE SIGNS IN STONES

"We thought he'd send the shot off before we got up the ladders!" exclaimed Dick. "We're expecting to hear the roar of it every minute now!"

"Perhaps something went wrong," suggested Will.

"What part of the mine is he in?" asked Jimmie.

Tommy explained the location of the cross-cutting and Jimmie gave a whistle of dismay. In a moment he asked:

"Was he cutting into one of the pillars?"

"Yes," was the answer; "he was getting ready to blow it down with dynamite. It's a wonder we don't hear the explosion!"

"If the spot where he's working is the place I think it is," Jimmie continued, "the gink stands a pretty good chance of finding something. We've been searching in that chamber, and just before you boys showed up tonight we thought we were on the right track. Whether the money is there or not, it is a sure thing that the walls of the chamber have been tampered with. We think, though, that the money is there!"

"Then we mustn't let Ventner get it!" exclaimed Will.

"It won't do him any good to get it after that stick of dynamite explodes!" exclaimed Tommy. "It'll blow him to Kingdom Come."

"Well, why don't we go down and see about it?" asked Will.

"Not for me!" exclaimed Tommy.

"He may blow his own head off if he wants to," Dick cut in, "but he can't blow off mine, not with my consent. I've got only one head!"

"I don't believe there's going to be any explosion at all!" exclaimed Elmer. "He wouldn't be apt to lay a fuse that would burn fifteen or twenty minutes, and you've certainly been that length of time coming up here, to say nothing of the time we've been talking!"

"All right!" Tommy exclaimed. "Perhaps he was loading up that pillar with dynamite just for the fun of it!"

"It would be a nice thing to have him blow that money out of the pillar and get away with it, wouldn't it?" scoffed Will.

"Come on, then," shouted Tommy, "I can take you to the firing line in about a minute. If you want to see an earthquake in a coal mine, just come along with me! You'll see it, all right!"

The boys left the old tool house without spending any more time in conversation, and hastened down the ladders to the lower level. On the way down the last gangway they heard some one moving about in the darkness, and then came a cry of warning.

"Stand clear! Stand clear!"

"That's Ventner's voice!" exclaimed Will.

"There's a blast going off in a minute!" the voice came again.

"Now we've gone and done it!" exclaimed Will. "After all the trouble we've taken to make that fellow think we've left the country, we've let him bump right into us. I wonder if he really has fired the fuse."

"Stand clear! Stand clear!" shouted the voice.

Almost before the words had died out, the explosion came, tearing more than one pillar out of position and dropping a great mass of slate down on the floor of the cross-cutting.

For a moment the gases which filled the chambers were overpowering. The only wonder was that they were not ignited. The electric lights carried by the boys shone dimly through the smoke of the confined place.

"There goes Ventner," whispered Will, pointing to a figure moving swiftly through the half-light of the place.

"He's going to see what the shot brought down!" suggested Tommy.

The boys rushed forward in a little group. When they gathered at the scene of the explosion, the detective was not there.

"If he got hold of the cash, he knew what to do with it all

right!" exclaimed Tommy. "He got away with it before we got a chance to see what he had. Now we've got to catch him!"

"May as well look for a needle in a load of hay!" grumbled Sandy.

"Look here," Jimmie exclaimed. "There's a way to keep him shut up in the mine if we do the right thing. This cross-cutting runs out to a gangway on the north, and that, in turn, leads, of course, to the shaft. Now, one of you boys duck out to the shaft and see that he doesn't get up. You'll have to go some on the way there, because a man with two hundred thousand dollars in his pocket will put up some running match!"

"I'm off!" shouted Tommy. "I know I can get to the shaft before he can! He's too fat-bellied to run, anyway!"

Tommy started away at a swift pace, and the other boys closed in on the gangway, Will alone stopping at the scene of the explosion.

"This gangway," Dick explained, "runs back into the mine for some distance, but there are no cross passages. I guess the coal wasn't very good here. At least, they never spread out the drive."

"Then we've got him bottled up unless he got out of the shaft!" declared Sandy. "We'll soon know whether he got out or not!"

"I don't believe he would try to get out," suggested Elmer. "The chances are that he'd make for the back of the mine, thinking to hide away with the plunder, provided he had any plunder to hide away with."

"I'm afraid he found the hidden money," Will said, taking a scorched ten-dollar bill from a pocket. "I found this back there, where the pillar fell. I guess he found the cash all right!"

"And that's a nice thing, too!" exclaimed Sandy. "You boys kept saying that Ventner was helping you find the coin. You were right about that, for he did find the coin. And now the trick is to get it away from him!"

"I'd like to know whether Ventner got up the shaft or not," suggested George, "and I believe I'll take a run up there and see.

"That's a good idea!" advised Will. "If he didn't get up the shaft he's surely imprisoned in the gangway. He may be between this cross-cutting and the shaft, or he may have gone further in!"

"It'll take a long time to find out about that," suggested Jimmie.

Directly Tommy and George were heard returning from the shaft. They came through the gangway flashing their lights in every direction.

"He never went up the shaft!" Tommy exclaimed as they came near. "We've got him canned in the mine all right. If he's got the money, we'll take it away from him! He wouldn't know what to do with it, anyway!"

"First," suggested Will, "we'd better make sure that the fellow got the money. The bank note I found may have never been in the possession of Mr. Carson. And even if it was, it may be the only one to be blown out of its hiding place by the explosion. It strikes me that we'd better give the place a thorough search before we waste much time looking for Ventner. If, as Tommy says, he never left the mine by way of the shaft, we've got him blocked in, all right!"

The boys now began a careful examination of the cross-cutting where the explosion had taken place. As has been stated, more than one pillar had been blown out. There was a great heap of debris on the floor, and this the boys attacked with a vim.

Tommy and George were now standing guard at the mouth of the cross-cutting so that no one could pass down the gangway toward the shaft.

"Suppose that fellow did get the money?" asked Sandy, as the boys cleared away the heaps of slate, "what then?"

"Then we'll have to take it away from him!"

"We'll catch him first."

"We've got him blocked in, haven't we?" asked Sandy.

"Oh, we know that he can't get out," Dick cut in, "but we know, too, that there are a lot of shallow benches along that gangway. We can't walk in and pick him out in a minute. Besides," the boy continued, "when we find him, we may find his pockets empty."

"That's just what we will do!" Elmer agreed. "He'll hide the money in another place, and swear that he never found it!"

"I wish we'd kicked him out of the mine!" exclaimed Sandy.

The boys continued their search until daylight, and then, leaving Tommy and George still on guard, they went up to the old tool house for breakfast. The lads were by no means elated over what had taken place. They believed that Ventner had succeeded in finding the money, and were certain that, even if located in the mine, he would deny any knowledge of it.

"I guess we got you boys into a mess by insisting on having the detective roaming around," admitted Elmer, as the boys were eating a hastily prepared breakfast. "I guess we should have listened to you in regard to that. There is no knowing how much trouble we have made!"

"He may help us find the money after all!" laughed Will.

"Yes," cut in Sandy, "it may be easier to get it away from him than to find the place where it was hidden."

"Oh, yes, if we could lay our hands on him and order him to give up two hundred thousand dollars, and he would say: 'Yes, I've been waiting to find the owner,' that would be all right, too! But the thing isn't likely to turn out in that way! He'll hide the money, and swear he never found it! Then, when everything quiets down, he'll sneak back and get it!"

This from Jimmie, who seemed to take a rather gloomy view of the situation. The boys remained at the old tool house only a short time. Their minds were fixed so intently on the work in hand that they hardly knew whether they had had any breakfast at all.

As they passed down the ladders to the lower level, they heard something which resembled a pistol shot, and almost tumbled over each other getting down into the gangway. Will and Elmer were first to reach the cross-heading where the explosion of dynamite had taken place.

They called to Tommy and George, but received no answer.

They walked for some distance down the gangway without hearing any sound indicating the presence of their companions, or of any one else.

"Now that's a funny thing!" exclaimed Will. "I don't see why those boys should go rambling about the mine at a time like this just for the fun of the thing!"

"They never did!" replied Elmer. "You remember the shot we heard!"

"It might not have been a shot!" suggested Will.

As the boy spoke he bent over and pointed to three stones lying on the floor of the gangway.

"There!" he said. "The boys have left a record. They not only point out the trail, but warn, us that there is danger in following it!"

V. T. Sherman

CHAPTER XVIII

TWO HOLD-UP MEN

"That's Boy Scout talk all right!" exclaimed Elmer.

"Yes, the three stones, piled one on top of the other, mean that there is danger in following the trail. I don't understand exactly what kind of danger can be threatening us, and so the only thing we can do is to go on and find out," Will said with a glance backward.

The other boys now came up and a short consultation was held. It was decided to leave Sandy and Dick at the point where the explosion had taken place, while Will, Elmer and Jimmie followed on down the gangway.

"Now whatever you do," warned Will as the two boys were left behind, "don't leave this gangway for a minute. If Ventner isn't out of the mine now, we don't want him to get out. He may have the money or he may not. That is one of the things no fellow can find out at this time, but whether he has or not, we want him to give an account of himself before he leaves the Labyrinth. He's got several important questions to answer."

The boys promised to watch the passage faithfully, and the

others passed on down the gangway, flashing their lights in every direction and making no pretense of moving quietly.

"Look here," Jimmie said after they had proceeded some distance into the mine and discovered nothing of importance, "I have in my possession a great idea! Want to hear about it?"

"Sure!" laughed Will.

"We're making too much noise."

"Making too much noise in order to attract the attention of a couple of lost youngsters?" asked Elmer.

"They're not lost!" insisted Jimmie. "They've been lured away or dragged away! We don't know how many men were in the mine with Ventner!"

"Well, produce your idea!" Elmer exclaimed.

"Well, my notion is that I ought to go on ahead of you boys, walking as quietly as possible and without a light. If there are people waiting to snare us, they'll naturally think we've bunched our forces and are all coming along together. Then, you see," he continued, "I'll be right in among them before they suspect that we have a skirmish line out."

"That's an all right notion, kid!" answered Will.

"Then I'll be on my way," Jimmie replied. "And if I need help at any time, I'll give the call of the pack!"

"But you mustn't do that unless you have to," Will cautioned, "because, the minute the cry is heard, everybody within eighty rods would know what's going on. Have you matches with you?"

The boy felt in the pockets of his coat and nodded.

"Well, then," he said, "if you want to signal, wet your hands and rub the phosphorus off the matches. Turn your hands, palms in our direction, so no one can see from the other side and wig-wag."

"That will be fine!" exclaimed Jimmie. "I've got this wig-wag system down pat. I guess this Boy Scout training is pretty poor, ain't it, eh? The darker it is, the better we can talk!"

Jimmie darted away, while Will and Elmer remained stationary for a short time in order to give him an opportunity to get out of the range of their lights. Directly they heard him whispering back and listened.

"There's another stone cairn here!" he said. "I guess I knocked it over, for I can't tell exactly what it is. You can learn that when you come up with your searchlights! I think there are three stones."

"All right!" Will whispered back.

When the boys came to the spot from which the voice had been heard they found three stones lying side by side on the floor of the gangway. It was plain that they had been placed one on top of the other, and so they accepted them as another warning of danger.

"I wish we had some intimation of the kind of trouble we are likely to get into," Elmer suggested, as they passed along. "I don't like this idea of boring a hole in the darkness with a little bit of a light and anticipating an attack at any minute."

"I don't like it a little bit myself," replied Will.

"A person so inclined might shoot us down without ever showing himself," declared Elmer. "In fact, the only protection we have lies in the fact that Jimmie is on ahead, and would not be likely to pass any one lying in wait for us. Bright little boy, that!"

"There he is now!" exclaimed Will. "He's using the phosphorus, all right, and I can begin to understand what he's trying to say? There's a 'W', and an 'A', and an 'I', and a 'T'. That means that he wants us to stay where we are. The system works fine, doesn't it?"

The question now was as to whether the lads should extinguish their lights. That, of itself, they understood would be suspicious in case they should be in sight of their enemies. It would simply proclaim their knowledge of the danger they were in, whatever it was.

"I think we'd better keep the lights going until we hear something more," Elmer said. "Jimmie will talk again in a minute."

The boys waited patiently for some moments, and then the wig-wag figures came again. Will read slowly:

"There's a 'V', and an 'E', and an 'N', and a 'T', and an 'N', and an 'E', and an 'R'," he said. "Now the boy's starting it again. He says, 'Ventner is here.' Now wait a minute, there's more coming!"

"The next words are: 'With two others'."

"It's only a question of time when that detective will get next to the wig-wag game," Elmer declared. "This gangway smells like a match factory already. I wonder how far Jimmie is away from them."

Directly Jimmie began talking the wig-wag tongue again. This time he said that Tommy and George were not in sight, and had evidently been surprised and taken prisoners. He advised Will and Elmer to come on softly with their lights out.

The boys did as requested, but they had advanced only a few paces in the darkness when Canfield, accompanied by Sandy and Dick came running up, showing both lack of breath and profound excitement.

"Boys," Canfield called. "Boys!"

"Will!" yelled Sandy.

"I guess they're going to bust up the whole combination!" declared Will rather sourly. "I wish I had them by the neck!"

"They may have important news," suggested Elmer. "Anyway, we'll have to turn on our lights and meet them. If we don't, they'll keep on yelling all down the gangway!"

Canfield and the two boys came up as soon as Elmer showed a light, and stood for a moment looking cautiously about.

"I don't think you boys ought to go any further into the mine!" Canfield exclaimed, breathing heavily from the long chase down the passage. "I have just received word that two of the most desperate hold-up men in the country have taken refuge here. There's no knowing how they got over to the mine, but it is a sure thing that they did get here, for a couple of breaker boys saw them climbing into the breaker."

"What time was this?" asked Will.

"Oh, I don't know," replied Canfield. "The matter was

reported to me early this morning. I couldn't find you before, or you should have had the news sooner. It isn't safe for you to go into the mine!"

"Your information," grinned Will, "comes a little bit late, but it's all right, just the same! Ventner is in there, and there are two men with, him. It's a mystery how they made their way in without being discovered, but it seems that they did so."

"What are you going to do?" asked Canfield.

"We're going on into the mine."

"In the face of my warning?"

"It's just this way," answered Will. "We left two of the boys on guard in this passage, not so very long ago, and they have disappeared. We suspect that Ventner and the two men to whom you refer have good reason to know something of their whereabouts."

"They won't injure the boys!" pleaded Canfield.

"We don't mean to give them a chance!" insisted Elmer. "We're going to jerk those boys out so quick it'll make their heads swim!"

"But it's positively dangerous!" urged the caretaker.

"If there wasn't an element of danger in the situation, we wouldn't be here!" replied Will. "I don't see as we need to run away from two hold-up men, anyway," the boy went on. "Here are five boys and one full grown man in the gangway. We ought to give a pretty good account of ourselves, in case some one starts anything!"

"Where's the fifth boy?" asked Canfield. "It seems to me that you're getting quite an accumulation of boys in here!"

"Two of the boys are Jimmie Maynard and Dick Thompson!" answered Will. "You know you informed me quite positively not long ago that the two lads were hundreds of miles from this place by this time."

"You might barricade the hold-up men and starve them out," suggested Canfield, "that is, if you're sure they're in there!"

"We have just had a wireless from the interior," Elmer answered. "There are three men in there, all right!"

"Well, it won't take any longer to starve three out than it would one!" declared Canfield.

"Yes," Elmer cut in, "and about the first time the hold-up men got good and hungry, they'd be sending out Tommy's ears or one of George's fingers just as a warning to us not to meddle with their appetites."

Before long Jimmie began wig-wagging again, but before any words could be formed the waiting boys heard a distant scuffle, a short, quick cry of alarm, and then the phosphorus-covered palms disappeared from sight.

"They've got Jimmie!" Elmer said in a tone of dismay.

"Well, what are we going to do?" demanded Sandy. "We've got to do something right away, and that's no story out of the dream book!"

"I don't suppose it would be of any use to rush them," suggested Elmer.

"They'd mow us down like rats!" declared Dick.

"It strikes me," Sandy said, "that we'd ought to get back further and keep out of sight until we can decide upon some definite plan of action."

"I've got an idea wandering around in the back of my brain," Will said. "If the situation is exactly as I think it is, we may be able to get the best of those hold-up men after all."

V. T. Sherman

CHAPTER XIX

THE MONEY IN SIGHT

"Not while they have possession of the boys," Canfield declared, dolefully. "They'll murder those boys if we shut off their supplies!"

"Oh, I don't know about that!" suggested Dick. "We've been mixed up in a great many awkward situations, but we've always managed to save our necks. We'll get the boys out in some way!"

"Look here, Mr. Canfield," Will said, "how well do you know this mine?"

"Every inch, of it!" was the reply.

"Every inch of every level," asked Will.

"Yes, sir!" replied the caretaker, rather proudly. "I can go into any part of it without a light!"

"Then look here, Dick," Will directed. "You chase back to the old tool house and bring back a long rope. And when you return, stop at the second level. Some of us will meet you there."

"I hope you don't expect to pull these boys up through fifty or a hundred feet of shale?" asked the caretaker.

"I don't know whether my scheme will work or not," Will answered, "but it's worth trying! We shall have to leave at least two here, well armed, and take the others with us. You'll have to act as guide, Mr. Canfield, and we'll meet Dick when he comes down to the second level with the rope. As soon as we get the boys out of their trouble, we can leave the three outlaws in full possession of the mine. If we watch the shaft at the old tool house, they can never get out without our knowing it!"

"I don't understand what you have in mind," faltered Canfield.

Leaving Sandy and Elmer in the gangway from which the wig-wag signals had been shown, the others hastened up the ladder to the second level. Then Dick ran away to bring the rope, while Will questioned the caretaker regarding the fall between the two levels.

"You remember the old shaft, cut through years ago, and doubtless deserted when the vein ran out, which at one time connected the two levels, don't you?" asked the boy of the caretaker.

"There is such a place," replied the caretaker.

"Can you find it?"

"Of course I can."

"Does the fall open into the system of chambers in the center or to the north? You understand what I mean! Is it possible to enter any of the benches or chambers connecting with the north gangway on the lower level by means of this deserted shaft?"

"I am not quite certain about that," replied Canfield, "but my idea is that the north benches and chambers can be reached by means of that opening. I am glad you thought of that," he went on.

Dick now returned with the rope, and the three proceeded down the second level until they came to a confusion of passages and benches which would certainly have bewildered any one not familiar with the mine.

"Unless I am very much mistaken," Canfield went on, "this passage, the one straight ahead, runs almost directly over Tunnel Six. If I am right in this, the deserted shaft is here."

"And Tunnel Six is the haunted corridor, isn't it?" asked Dick.

"That's where the lights have been seen!" replied the caretaker.

"You never believed in the ghost stories told about Tunnel Six?" asked Will. "I should think you'd begin to see now that the alleged ghosts were pretty material things."

"Well, I don't know about the ghosts," replied the caretaker, "but I really was getting a little bit nervous when you boys arrived. You know," he continued, "that we all feel a little shivery when we butt into anything which we can't understand."

"Well, suppose you follow this passage to the end and see if you discover anything like the deserted shaft," suggested Dick.

"You're not going to venture into the lower level again, are you?" asked Canfield. "I don't blame you boys for wanting to rescue your companions, but, at the same time, I don't want to see you throw your lives away. Those are desperate men in Tunnel Six!"

"If my idea is worth anything at all," replied Will, "we'll get the boys out without ever letting the hold-up men know that we are within a mile of them. You know we had very little difficulty in getting out of the chamber where we left the boat."

"Trust you boys for inventing ways of doing things!" exclaimed Canfield.

"Of course," Will said hesitatingly after a time, "it may be that this deserted shaft doesn't connect with Tunnel Six, but even if it doesn't, we'll find some way of getting to our friends from the new position. We can only try, anyway!"

"I'm pretty certain that it connects with Tunnel Six," replied the caretaker. "But you mustn't show your light when you approach the old shaft," he went on, "because if it does connect with the chamber we seek, and the chamber in turn connects with the north passage, the robbers will see what we're doing."

"That's a valuable suggestion!" replied Will.

"I'll go on ahead," Canfield continued, "and find the old shaft. Then you can follow on with the rope, and one of you boys can drop down and see what can be discovered."

"It's dollars to apples," chuckled Dick, as the boys trailed along after the caretaker, "that we find the three kids trussed up like a lot of hens ready for the market in the chamber where you came so near getting wet. I hope we do, at any rate!"

"There's one thing we overlooked," Will said as Canfield whispered to them that he had found the deserted shaft, "and that is this: We should have directed the boys in the gangway to have attracted the attention of the outlaws by a little pistol practice while we are communicating with our friends. They may be all packed away in the chamber together."

"Yes, we should have attended to that," replied Dick. "Perhaps I'd better go back now and tell them to get busy with their automatics."

"We may as well investigate the situation here first," the other answered.

The boys heard the caretaker creeping about in the darkness, and presently a piece of shale or coal was heard rattling down the old shaft.

"We'll have to get that blundering caretaker away from there," whispered Will. "If we don't, he'll notify the hold-up men that we're getting ready to do something! I've heard that about three-fourths of the people in the world object to doing anything unless they can take a brass band along, and I guess it's true."

"Say," Canfield whispered, calling back to the lads, "when that stone dropped down, I heard something that sounded like a paddle slapping down on the water. That room can't be wet yet, can it?"

"The Beaver call!" whispered Will.

"Right you are!" replied Dick. "The boys are there, all right!"

"Now the next thing to do is to find out if those highwaymen are watching them," declared Will.

"I'll tell you that in a minute," Dick whispered.

As the boy spoke, he passed one end of the rope to Canfield.

"Hang on to it, whatever takes place!" he whispered, "and I'll drop down and see what's going on."

"You must be very careful," warned Canfield.

"That's all right," answered Dick, "but we can't stand here all day figuring out precautions. We've got to know right off whether there's anyone in that chamber watching the boys!"

"What a joke it would be to put on a ghost in Tunnel Six!" laughed Will, in a decidedly cheerful frame of mind, now that rescue seemed so near.

"Don't try any foolishness!" advised Canfield. "Let's rescue the boys if possible and make our way out of this horrible place."

Will crawled to the edge of the shaft with Dick and whispered as he lowered him into the dark opening below:

"Remember," he said, "that Ventner may have discovered the money. If so, we must secure it before we leave the place! It will be just like him to stow the bank notes away in some chamber like the one you are about to enter. When you strike bottom, if there is no one in sight except the boys, turn on your searchlight and take a good look over the interior of the chamber.

"We were in there not so very long ago, but at that time we

150   V. T. Sherman

weren't thinking of making a search there for hidden money. You'll have to use your own judgment about turning on the light, of course. The outlaws may be out in the gangway, some distance from the entrance to the chamber, or they may be within six feet of where the boys are held as prisoners."

"Tommy ought to be able to tell me the minute I strike the heap of shale whether the outlaws are close by or not!" Dick suggested.

"Of course!" answered Will, "if he knows. If the men are not in sight, and he doesn't know where they are, you'll simply have to take chances. If you get caught in there, you'll have to shoot, and shoot quick!"

Dick, dropped down into the old shaft and directly the anxious watchers above heard the rattle of shale as it dropped from the pyramid under the opening. Will, still clinging to the rope, lay on his stomach and peered downward, watching with all anxiety for some show of light, or some sound which might indicate the situation below.

Directly Will felt a soft, steady pull at the rope, and knew that one of the boys was ready to be assisted to the top.

Dick came up first, chuckling as he landed on the edge of the break in the rock, and was immediately followed by Jimmie.

"Where's Tommy and George?" asked Will in a whisper.

"They're down there looking for the money!"

"Looking for the money in the darkness?"

"Sure!" was the reply. "You see," he went on, "those ginks tied us up good and tight, and then threw the money around promiscuous like!"

"So the money is there?" asked Will.

The news seemed too good to be true!

"It was there when we were first thrown into the chamber," replied Jimmie, "but I have an idea that Ventner sneaked in and removed it so as to prevent his mates getting any share."

A light flashed out from below, followed immediately by a pistol shot!

CHAPTER XX

SANDY IS DISCHARGED

Elmer and Sandy, guarding the gangway variously called the North section and Tunnel Six, presently heard voices coming from the direction of the shaft, and the latter moved back a few paces in order to inspect the new-comers. In a moment he saw three rather pompous looking men approaching him, their footsteps being directed by a man clothed as a miner.

"Here, boy!" shouted one of the pompous men. "Can you tell me where Canfield, the caretaker of this mine, may be found?"

"He's up on the next level," replied Sandy.

"I was told he was down here," growled the speaker, who was very short and fat, and very much out of breath.

"He was here a little while ago," answered Sandy.

"What's the meaning of this show of firearms?" demanded the fat man, after glancing disdainfully at the automatic in the boy's hand.

"We've got three robbers cooped up in the mine,"

replied Sandy.

"That's the old, old story!" exclaimed the fat man. "I don't know that I ever knew of a mine that wasn't haunted, either by ghosts or robbers! Mysteries seem to breed in coal mines!"

Sandy walked back to the place where he had left Elmer, and the three men and their guide followed him. When Elmer caught a view of the fat man's face and figure, he gave a sharp pull at Sandy's sleeve.

"That's Stephen Carson!" he said. "I guess I'd better keep out of sight, because I don't care about getting into an argument with him. He's the most contrary person I ever saw in my life, and never fails to get up an argument about something or other with yours truly."

"You seem to know him pretty well," whispered Sandy.

"I ought to," returned Elmer, "he's my Uncle! The two tall men in the party are my father and the cashier of the Night and Day bank. I'll take a sneak, and that will shorten the session."

Accordingly, Elmer strolled along the gangway and came to a halt some distance from where the three men had drawn up.

"My boy," Carson went on, looking condescendingly at the youth, "will you kindly run up to the second level and tell Mr. Canfield that his presence is required by the president of the mining company?"

"I'm not allowed to leave this place, sir," replied Sandy, taking offense at the man's air of proprietorship.

"All persons in and about this mine," Carson almost shouted, "are subject to my orders. Run along now, you foolish boy, find don't make any further trouble for yourself!"

The man's manner was so unnecessarily dictatorial and offensive that Sandy found it impossible to retain his temper. He was not naturally a "fresh" youngster, but now he had passed the limit of endurance.

"Aw, go chase yourself!" he said.

"You're discharged!" shouted Carson.

"You didn't hire me!" retorted Sandy. "You haven't got any right to discharge me! I'm going to stay here until I get ready to leave!"

"If you don't get out of the mine immediately, I'll have you thrown out!" shouted Carson. "I never saw such impudence!"

"If I do get out," replied Sandy with a grin, "you'll wish I hadn't!"

Carson turned to Elmer's father and the bank cashier, and the three consulted together for a short time. Then Elmer's father came closer to where Sandy was standing.

"Why do you say that?" he asked. "Why do you think we will wish you had remained in case you are sent out of the mine?"

"Because I was left here to prevent robbers getting out of the gangway. They're further in, and have captured three of my chums."

"All nonsense!" shouted Mr. Carson breaking into the

conversation impatiently. "These breaker boys never tell the truth!"

"Are you Mr. Buck?" asked Sandy, speaking in an undertone to Elmer's father. "Because if you are, you'll find Elmer just a short distance ahead. He's on guard, too. He didn't want his uncle to recognize him, because he says he's always getting up an argument with him."

"I'm glad to know that Elmer is attending to his duty," Mr. Buck answered. "Somehow," he continued with a smile, "Stephen Carson always rubs Elmer the wrong way of the grain."

"What's he butting in here for?" asked Sandy, while the cashier of the Night and Day bank and the miner stood by waiting for the peace negotiations to conclude.

"Why, he came in to get his two hundred thousand dollars!" replied Mr. Buck. "He thinks he knows How right where he left it."

"Does he often get foolish in the head like that?" asked Sandy with a grin. "If he does, he ought to hire a couple of detectives to keep track of him when he goes wandering out in the night!"

"Oh, Stephen is usually a pretty level-headed sort of a fellow!" replied Mr. Buck. "He is out of humor just now because he has always denied that he visited the mine during his two weeks of absence. He is one of the men who dislike very much to be caught in an error of any kind."

"So he knows where the money is?" asked Sandy.

"He says he can find it if he can secure the services of

Canfield, the caretaker. He remembers now of getting in the mine, and of hearing footsteps in the darkness. His impression at that time was that robbers had followed him in, so he unloaded the banknotes in a small chamber which he is now able to describe accurately but which he cannot, of course, find."

"Was the money hidden on this level?" asked Sandy.

"Yes, on this level."

"In this gangway?"

"He thinks it was hidden here."

"Right about here, or further on?"

"Why," was the answer, "he seems to remember something about Tunnel Six. He thinks he hid the money there! As soon as he finds Canfield, the caretaker will probably be able to tell him exactly how Tunnel Six looks."

"It looks all in a mess right now! I can tell you that," grinned Sandy.

"What do you mean by that?"

"I mean that there's been doings here!" replied Sandy.

"Are there really robbers in there?"

"Sure, there are robbers in there!"

"Then perhaps we'd better bring in a squad of deputies."

"If you'll just let us boys alone," Sandy said, "we'll bring the money out if it's anywhere in the mine, but if this man Carson goes to butting in at this time, he'll have to dig out his own money. He won't believe there's any robbers in there, and he wants to fire me out of the mine, so I guess we'd better let him go his own gait a little while."

"He'll do that anyhow no matter what you say!" replied Mr. Buck.

"Look here!" shouted Carson, starting forward, with his stomach out and his fat shoulders thrown back, "what's all this conversation about? Why don't some one go up and get Canfield, and why isn't that young rowdy thrown out of the mine? I won't have him in here!"

"Say," Sandy broke in, "Mr. Buck says that you're looking for Tunnel Six. If you are, I can show you right where it is!"

"Do so, then!" shouted Carson.

"Go straight ahead," Sandy directed, "and when the robbers begin to shoot, you command them to throw down their weapons in the name of the law. They'll probably do it, all right, if you tell them to, but you'll be lucky if they don't throw them down your throat!"

"Do you mean to tell me," screamed Carson, "that there are actually robbers here, and that they have taken possession of Tunnel Six?"

"That's the idea," replied Sandy.

"Why, that's where I put my—"

"That's where you put your money, is it?" Sandy went on.

V. T. Sherman

"I never saw such impudence!" reared Carson.

"Well, go on and get your money!" advised Sandy. "Just go straight down the gangway until you come to a face of rock and then switch off to the left, and you'll find yourself in a chamber used at present by robbers and hold-up men as a winter resort."

"Oh you can't frighten me!" declared Carson. "I believe that you're here in quest of the money yourself!"

"That's right!" admitted Sandy. "Go on in, now, and tell the robbers to give up your hoarded gold! Just butt in, and tell 'em what you want them to do! They'll probably do just as you tell them to!"

"I never saw such impudence in my life!" roared Carson, wiping his perspiring forehead with a large red silk handkerchief.

"I don't see where the impudence comes in!" replied Sandy. "You said you wanted to find Tunnel Six in order that you might locate your money. I'm telling you where it is, and what to do to get it!"

"Old Stephen never took a bluff in his life!" chuckled Mr. Buck, "Now see if he doesn't go stalking down that passage and declaring himself in the name of the law!"

The banker did exactly what Mr. Buck had predicted. He went storming down the passage, giving notice to all intruders to walk out of his mine in a peaceable manner. Mr. Buck followed along until he came to where Elmer was standing with his back against the wall, and then the two paused and entered into conversation. The cashier of the Night and Day bank and the miner started back toward the shaft.

"What's the matter?" shouted Sandy. "Why don't you stay and see the fun? There'll be shooting here directly!"

The miner and the cashier now took to their heels and were soon out of sight. Every moment the boy expected to see a flash of fire in the gangway. Carson was now very near to Tunnel Six, and it seemed certain that the outlaws must soon open fire on him.

"Come back, Stephen!" shouted Mr. Buck. "Don't make a fool of yourself!"

"This is all pure bluff!" shouted Carson. "There are no robbers here at all. This is a scheme to keep me out of Tunnel Six, where I believe my money to be hidden!"

They saw Carson halt in his rather clumsy passage down the gangway, and draw an automatic revolver from his pocket.

There was a quick shot and the banker rushed ahead!

V. T. Sherman

CHAPTER XXI

"I TOLD YOU SO!"

Directly Elmer, Sandy and Mr. Buck heard the banker shouting at the top of his lungs and dashed on toward the mysterious tunnel.

"He'll get his head shot off in there!" exclaimed Sandy.

"I don't care if he does!" declared Elmer.

"Your uncle isn't such a bad old fellow, after all," Mr. Buck exclaimed. "He has plenty of courage, at any rate!"

"But I don't understand why they don't open fire on him!" exclaimed Sandy. "The robbers certainly were in there not very long ago. We heard the scuffle when they geezled Jimmie."

"Who fired that shot?" asked Mr. Buck.

"Uncle Stephen did," replied Elmer. "I saw the flash spring out from the spot where he stood!"

"Well, what do you know about that?" exclaimed Sandy. "The old chap is actually making his bluff good! He's getting into Tunnel Six single handed and alone! I guess we'll have to advertise for those three outlaws if we find 'em in here! He's a nervy old fellow, isn't he?"

The three now followed fast on the heels of the banker, and soon came to where he stood swinging his searchlight at the end of a short drift which ended, after sliding under a dip, in a chamber which at first glance seemed to be piled high with a mass of shale.

While the three looked on, Carson dropped on his knees beside a crevice in the wall and began an eager exploration of the opening.

Directly he sprang to his feet with rage and disappointment showing on every feature of his face. He raved about the cluttered chamber for a moment, almost dancing up and down in his anger and chagrin, and then sat limply down on the pile of shale.

"It's gone!" he said. "The money's gone!"

"So it wasn't hidden back there in that cross-cutting at all?" asked Sandy. "We thought sure we had a cinch on the coin several hours ago!"

"It was hidden here in this chamber!" declared Carson wearily. "The minute I entered the place I remembered where I had hidden it. And now it's gone! I've had all my trouble for nothing."

As he ceased speaking, he glanced suspiciously at Sandy. And Sandy, in turn, made a most provoking face.

"I believe you know something about my money!" Carson said.

"Sure I do!" replied Sandy.

"Then where is it?"

"The robbers got it!"

"That's a nice story to tell," howled Carson. "If you think I'm going to be defrauded out of my money in this way, you're very much mistaken!"

Without paying any further attention to the threats of the banker, Sandy stepped over to Elmer's side and pointed up the deserted shaft.

"There's where the robbers went," he said, "and they doubtless took Carson's money with them. I don't understand why Will didn't stop them."

"Will and George probably released their friends and went away," complained Elmer. "I don't think they showed very good judgment in doing that, either. The result is that the money has now disappeared entirely. A short time ago, Uncle might have reclaimed it."

"We don't know whether the money has gone beyond recall or not," replied Sandy. "I don't believe Will and George ever left the old shaft unguarded. They are still somewhere in this vicinity!"

Carson now blustered up to Sandy and pointed an accusing finger into the lad's face. Sandy regarded him with indifference.

"Now that your story of the robbers has been disproved," Carson shouted, "you may as well tell me who took my money. If I had not the courage to make this investigation in person, that cheap story of the robbers would have held good for all time!"

"That's a horse on me, all right!" admitted Sandy. "I don't know where the robbers are, unless they went up through that old shaft, and it doesn't seem as if the boys would permit that!"

"Too thin! Entirely too thin!" declared Carson. "A moment ago you tried to tell me that the money wasn't hidden near Tunnel Six at all, but was hidden back there near the cross-cutting."

"We had good reason to believe it was hidden there!" replied Sandy. "We found a burned ten-dollar banknote there just after a dynamite explosion had taken place."

"That would naturally lead to the supposition that the money had been hidden there!" Mr. Buck exclaimed.

"Come to think of it," Sandy went on, "I believe that was one of Ventner's tricks. I believe he blew down those pillars and burned the banknote for the express purpose of making us search two or three weeks in the wrong place. I guess we have under-estimated that fellow's ability. He's a keener man than I supposed!"

"I don't quite see the point to that," Elmer suggested. "When you say that Ventner probably caused you to dig in the wrong place, you admit that he must have known something about the right place. Now, how could he have known anything about where to look for that money?"

"I don't know," replied Sandy. "But when you say that he might have known exactly where to look, you set him down as a fool, because he has been searching a long time and never came upon it until today."

"I think I can understand that," Mr. Buck said. "This man you speak of probably knew where to find the money provided he could discover the right drift, bench, chamber or tunnel. Like Mr. Carson, here, he could doubtless go straight to the cache if directed into the right apartment."

While the four stood together at the bottom of the chamber, their searchlights making the place as light as day, an exclamation came from the shaft above, followed by two pistol shots.

Carson dropped to his knees and began twisting at his automatic, which had in some way become entangled in the lining of his pocket.

"There are your robbers!" he shouted. "Put out your lights!"

"Don't you do anything of the kind!" argued Sandy. "Get out of range of the old shaft and keep your lights burning so you can shoot any one who drops down! I guess we have them hemmed in!"

"It's a scheme to get away with my money!" shouted Carson.

"I wish you had your old money chucked down your throat!" exclaimed Sandy. "I'm getting sick of the sound of the word!"

All members of the party now drew back toward the dip, where they were entirely concealed from any one in the old shaft.

Directly there was a rattling of shale and slate, and then the lights showed the figure of Tommy sitting astride the peak of the pyramid.

"What you fellows trying to do down there?" he asked.

"We're looking for Carson's money?" replied Sandy.

"Did you get it?" the boy demanded.

"Not yet!"

"That's the boy that's got my money!" shouted the banker.

"Money's a good thing to have!" grinned Tommy.

"What have you done with the highwaymen?" asked Sandy.

"Why continue this senseless talk about highwaymen?" demanded Carson, "when you know just as well as I do that there are no robbers here other than yourselves! Mr. Buck," he added, turning to Elmer's father, "I call upon you to assist me in restraining these robbers until the proper officers can be summoned."

"Where did that fat man come from?" asked Tommy.

"You impertinent rascal!" shouted Carson.

"Sure!" answered Tommy. "But where did you say you came from?"

"I'm president of this mining company!" screamed Carson, "and I'll have you all in jail if you don't produce my money!"

"Is this the gentleman who went batty and lost two hundred thousand dollars?" asked Tommy, sliding down from the slate pyramid and standing beside Sandy.

"That is believed to be the man!" laughed Sandy.

"Believed to be!" roared Carson.

"Does he know where he left the money?" asked Tommy.

"Sure I know where I left my money, you young jackanapes!" declared Carson. "I pointed out the exact hiding place only a few moments ago!"

"You found it empty?"

"Yes, I found it empty," roared Carson.

"Then," Tommy suggested, "we've all got to get busy."

"What do you mean by that?" demanded Carson.

Before Tommy could reply, Will came sliding down the rope and landed within a few feet of where the little group stood.

"Look here, Will," Tommy said, "are you sure we made a good search of those three ginks? They've got the money all right!"

"How do you know they did?" demanded Will.

"That fat man over there who looks as if he was about to bust," Tommy grinned, "is Mr. Carson, the man who hid the money and couldn't find it again. He's just been looking in the place where he concealed it, and it isn't there! We've got to get busy!"

"I don't understand this at all," Mr. Buck interrupted.

"It's just this way," Will said, facing the speaker "we caught the three men who were wandering about in the mine. We rescued our chums first, and then when the outlaws heard your party advancing they scrambled up the old shaft and took to their heels, supposing, of course, that we had lost no time in getting out of the mine."

"And you geezled them all?" asked Sandy.

"The whole three!" replied Will. "All we had to do was to stretch a rope across a passage, trip them up, and do a little winding around their great big forms before they could get their breath. They're all tied up good and tight now."

"And you searched them for the money and didn't find it?" shouted Carson.

"And we searched them for the money and didn't find it!" repeated Will.

"I don't believe it!" shouted Carson. "You'll be telling me in a moment, when I ask you to produce your robbers, that they have broken their bonds and escaped!"

At that moment, George's voice was heard calling down the shaft:

"Break for the main shaft!" they heard him saying. "Head those fellows off! They cut their ropes and got away!"

"I told you so!" thundered Carson.

V. T. Sherman

CHAPTER XXII

CONCLUSION

"Bright boys up there!" exclaimed Will, as the unwelcome news of the escape of the robbers came down the old shaft.

"Me for the elevator!" shouted Tommy.

All four boys, Will, Elmer, Tommy and Sandy, started in a mad race down the gangway. As they carried their search-lights with them, and as Mr. Carson and Mr. Buck moved at a slower pace, the latter gentlemen were soon feeling their way through a dark tunnel.

"We've just got to head 'em off!" grunted Tommy, as the boys passed along at a pace calculated to break the long distance running records.

"I don't believe they'll make for the main shaft anyway," Sandy panted.

"I don't believe they will, either," Will declared, "but if we get to the lift first, we'll be dead sure they don't get out!"

Will was in advance as they swung into the lighted space about the shaft. The first thing he observed was that one of the cages was just starting upward. He sprang to the push button and almost instantly the cage dropped back to the third level again. The power was on in honor of the visit of the president of the company.

"Pile in, boys!" he shouted. "We'll stop at the second level!"

The man at the top responded nobly to the quick signals given to start and stop, and in a very short space of time the elevator stood at the second level. The bar was down, but Will threw it aside and stepped out into the passage. There he saw the bank cashier and the miner standing cowering against the wall only a few feet from the shaft.

"What are you doing here?" asked Will.

"We started to the top," the miner replied, "but stopped here because we thought there might be need of our assistance on this level."

"Why on this level?" asked Will, observing that the miner was pretty thoroughly frightened. "I haven't heard of any disturbance here!"

"But there has been a disturbance here!" insisted the cashier. "We heard scuffling out there in the darkness, but as we had no lights, we could not investigate. My friend, the miner, had a light on the lower level, but he lost it as we made our way out to the shaft."

"Has any one passed up the shaft?" asked Will.

The miner shook his head.

"Then we're in time all right!" cried Will exultantly. "We have the outlaws headed off!"

The heavy voices of the two men who had been left on the lower level now came rumbling up the shaft.

"What do you mean by leaving us in this plight?" demanded Carson. "Lower the cage instantly, and take us to the top!"

"Stay down there and look after your money!" cried Sandy, mockingly.

"I think I know where my money is!" shouted Carson.

"I wish I knew!" returned Sandy.

In the moment of silence which followed the boys heard the call of the Beaver Patrol ringing down the second level.

"George seems to be alive anyway!" laughed Tommy.

A moment later a snarling sound which seemed to emanate from a whole pack of Wolves reached the ears of the boys.

"Why didn't you tell me there were wild animals in the mine?" shouted the cashier. "Let me into that cage immediately!"

"Don't be in a hurry," advised Tommy. "All the Wolves and Beavers you'll find in here won't do you any harm!"

While Carson and Elmer's father continued to call from below, and while the Boy Scout challenges rang in the second level, two pistol shots were heard not far away from the shaft.

The cashier and the miner both broke for the cage, but were turned back at the point of Sandy's automatic revolver.

"You stopped here because you thought you might be of some assistance, you know," the boy said. "Now you just remain here long enough to help out."

"But there are people being murdered in there!" cried the cashier.

Two more shots came from the gangway and then the stout figure of the detective came staggering into the circle of light around the shaft. He had evidently been wounded seriously, for he fell as he drew near to where the boys were standing and raised his eyes in a piteous appeal for help. Will stooped over and felt of his pulse.

"You're about done for!" the boy said in a husky tone. "Who did it?"

"Those two hold-up men," was the faint reply.

"Where are they now?" asked Will.

"I fired back," replied the detective with a grim smile, "and I guess they're lying on the floor of the passage!"

Will bent closer over the wounded detective while Tommy and Sandy started down the gangway on a run, closely followed by Elmer.

"Why did they shoot you?" asked Will.

"I found the money," Ventner replied, "and hid it in a crevice in the wall, and they found it. When we managed to escape by cutting the ropes I saw them take the money and disappear in the darkness. I followed on and accused them of the act and they shot me! Then I shot back, and I guess it's a pretty bad mess, when you take it altogether!"

"Where is the money?" asked Will.

"They have it in their possession," was the reply, "if they haven't hidden it again."

Before the wounded detective could continue, George, Jimmie, Dick, Canfield, Sandy and Tommy came running out of the gangway.

"Where's Elmer?" asked Will.

"We left him back there talking with one of the hold-up men," replied George. "They're both badly hurt, and won't last long!"

"I'm not sorry!" moaned Ventner.

A moment later, Elmer came out of the passage with a bill-book of good size in his hand. He lifted the book gaily as he entered the illumination.

"I'll bet he's got the money!" exclaimed Tommy.

"Sure he has!" replied Will, and Elmer nodded.

The voices of Carson and Buck again came roaring up from below.

"Why don't you lower the cage?" Carson shouted. "I'm going to have every one of you arrested as soon as I can find an officer! You can't work any of your gold brick schemes on me!"

"We may as well drop down and take them aboard," Will laughed.

Carson was swelling with rage when he stepped onto the platform of the list. He shook his fist fiercely under Will's nose, and announced that he would have him wearing handcuffs before night.

"How much reward was offered for the return of that two hundred thousand dollars?" asked the boy, without paying any attention to the angry demonstrations of the banker.

"Twenty thousand dollars!" replied Carson. "But you'll never get a cent of it. I hired a party of Boy Scouts to come here from Chicago and look into the case, but they never came near me."

"When you write to Chicago again," Will replied, with a smile as the elevator stopped at the second level, "just tell Mr. Horton that the Beaver's didn't succeed in getting the money, but that the Wolves did. Elmer has the money in his possession right this minute!"

"Impossible!" shouted Carson.

"Hand him the money, Elmer," requested Will.

Carson snatched the bill book as it was held out to him and began looking through the ten-thousand-dollar banknotes which it contained.

"The next time you get drunk and fall out of your machine, don't accuse every one you meet of robbing you!" Sandy cut in.

"Are you the boys who came on from Chicago?" demanded Carson.

"Sure!" replied Will.

"I guess I'm an old fool!" admitted Carson. "Here I've been roaming around about half a day accusing you boys of stealing my money, when all the time you were planning on returning it to me!"

"Do we get the reward now?" asked Will.

"Twenty thousand and expenses!" replied Carson. "I'll settle with Elmer and his chums later on!"

"It's a shame to take the money!" declared Sandy, but Will gave him a sharp punch in the back and he cut off any further remarks which he might have had in his mind.

The story ends here because the adventure ended with the finding of the money. The old tool house was deserted that night. The two hold-up men and the detective recovered after a long illness in a Pittsburgh hospital. The detective was permitted to go his way after promising to keep out of crooked detective deals in the future. He never told how or where he received his information about the lost money. The hold-up men were given long sentences in prison.

A few weeks later, when the mining company resumed operations at the Labyrinth, Tunnel Six was walled up. Mr. Carson, the president, declared that it made what few hairs he had left stand on end to think of the experiences he had endured there!

However, there are still stories about the breaker, that on dark nights, when the wind blows, and the rain falls in great sheets, there are mysterious lights floating about Tunnel Six.

Jimmie and Dick often tell exactly how these lights were made, and how they enjoyed themselves living down in the bowels of the earth, but the superstitious miners still claim that the boys were not responsible for all the lights which burned there!

Dick and Jimmie also have their joke with the Beaver Patrol boys whenever they meet, declaring that if they had not finally relented and dropped the string the boys had carried into the mine for their own protection, they would still be wandering around in the Labyrinth Mine.

"And now," Will said as they settled down in their old room on Washington boulevard, "we're going to be good boys from this time on and remain in Chicago and stay at home nights!"

However, in three days, the boys were preparing for another bit of adventure, the details of which will be found in the next volume of this series entitled:

"Boy Scouts in Alaska; or, The Camp on the Glacier."

The End

　　　　　　V. T. Sherman

Choose from Thousands of 1stWorldLibrary Classics By

A. M. Barnard
Ada Leverson
Adolphus William Ward
Aesop
Agatha Christie
Alexander Aaronsohn
Alexander Kielland
Alexandre Dumas
Alfred Gatty
Alfred Ollivant
Alice Duer Miller
Alice Turner Curtis
Alice Dunbar
Allen Chapman
Alleyne Ireland
Ambrose Bierce
Amelia E. Barr
Amory H. Bradford
Andrew Lang
Andrew McFarland Davis
Andy Adams
Angela Brazil
Anna Alice Chapin
Anna Sewell
Annie Besant
Annie Hamilton Donnell
Annie Payson Call
Annie Roe Carr
Annonaymous
Anton Chekhov
Archibald Lee Fletcher
Arnold Bennett
Arthur C. Benson
Arthur Conan Doyle
Arthur M. Winfield
Arthur Ransome
Arthur Schnitzler
Arthur Train
Atticus
B.H. Baden-Powell
B. M. Bower
B. C. Chatterjee
Baroness Emmuska Orczy
Baroness Orczy
Basil King
Bayard Taylor
Ben Macomber
Bertha Muzzy Bower
Bjornstjerne Bjornson

Booth Tarkington
Boyd Cable
Bram Stoker
C. Collodi
C. E. Orr
C. M. Ingleby
Carolyn Wells
Catherine Parr Traill
Charles A. Eastman
Charles Amory Beach
Charles Dickens
Charles Dudley Warner
Charles Farrar Browne
Charles Ives
Charles Kingsley
Charles Klein
Charles Hanson Towne
Charles Lathrop Pack
Charles Romyn Dake
Charles Whibley
Charles Willing Beale
Charlotte M. Braeme
Charlotte M. Yonge
Charlotte Perkins Stetson
Clair W. Hayes
Clarence Day Jr.
Clarence E. Mulford
Clemence Housman
Confucius
Coningsby Dawson
Cornelis DeWitt Wilcox
Cyril Burleigh
D. H. Lawrence
Daniel Defoe
David Garnett
Dinah Craik
Don Carlos Janes
Donald Keyhoe
Dorothy Kilner
Dougan Clark
Douglas Fairbanks
E. Nesbit
E. P. Roe
E. Phillips Oppenheim
E. S. Brooks
Earl Barnes
Edgar Rice Burroughs
Edith Van Dyne
Edith Wharton

Edward Everett Hale
Edward J. O'Biren
Edward S. Ellis
Edwin L. Arnold
Eleanor Atkins
Eleanor Hallowell Abbott
Eliot Gregory
Elizabeth Gaskell
Elizabeth McCracken
Elizabeth Von Arnim
Ellem Key
Emerson Hough
Emilie F. Carlen
Emily Bronte
Emily Dickinson
Enid Bagnold
Enilor Macartney Lane
Erasmus W. Jones
Ernie Howard Pie
Ethel May Dell
Ethel Turner
Ethel Watts Mumford
Eugene Sue
Eugenie Foa
Eugene Wood
Eustace Hale Ball
Evelyn Everett-green
Everard Cotes
F. H. Cheley
F. J. Cross
F. Marion Crawford
Fannie E. Newberry
Federick Austin Ogg
Ferdinand Ossendowski
Fergus Hume
Florence A. Kilpatrick
Fremont B. Deering
Francis Bacon
Francis Darwin
Frances Hodgson Burnett
Frances Parkinson Keyes
Frank Gee Patchin
Frank Harris
Frank Jewett Mather
Frank L. Packard
Frank V. Webster
Frederic Stewart Isham
Frederick Trevor Hill
Frederick Winslow Taylor

Friedrich Kerst
Friedrich Nietzsche
Fyodor Dostoyevsky
G.A. Henty
G.K. Chesterton
Gabrielle E. Jackson
Garrett P. Serviss
Gaston Leroux
George A. Warren
George Ade
Geroge Bernard Shaw
George Cary Eggleston
George Durston
George Ebers
George Eliot
George Gissing
George MacDonald
George Meredith
George Orwell
George Sylvester Viereck
George Tucker
George W. Cable
George Wharton James
Gertrude Atherton
Gordon Casserly
Grace E. King
Grace Gallatin
Grace Greenwood
Grant Allen
Guillermo A. Sherwell
Gulielma Zollinger
Gustav Flaubert
H. A. Cody
H. B. Irving
H.C. Bailey
H. G. Wells
H. H. Munro
H. Irving Hancock
H. R. Naylor
H. Rider Haggard
H. W. C. Davis
Haldeman Julius
Hall Caine
Hamilton Wright Mabie
Hans Christian Andersen
Harold Avery
Harold McGrath
Harriet Beecher Stowe
Harry Castlemon
Harry Coghill
Harry Houidini

Hayden Carruth
Helent Hunt Jackson
Helen Nicolay
Hendrik Conscience
Hendy David Thoreau
Henri Barbusse
Henrik Ibsen
Henry Adams
Henry Ford
Henry Frost
Henry James
Henry Jones Ford
Henry Seton Merriman
Henry W Longfellow
Herbert A. Giles
Herbert Carter
Herbert N. Casson
Herman Hesse
Hildegard G. Frey
Homer
Honore De Balzac
Horace B. Day
Horace Walpole
Horatio Alger Jr.
Howard Pyle
Howard R. Garis
Hugh Lofting
Hugh Walpole
Humphry Ward
Ian Maclaren
Inez Haynes Gillmore
Irving Bacheller
Isabel Cecilia Williams
Isabel Hornibrook
Israel Abrahams
Ivan Turgenev
J.G.Austin
J. Henri Fabre
J. M. Barrie
J. M. Walsh
J. Macdonald Oxley
J. R. Miller
J. S. Fletcher
J. S. Knowles
J. Storer Clouston
J. W. Duffield
Jack London
Jacob Abbott
James Allen
James Andrews
James Baldwin

James Branch Cabell
James DeMille
James Joyce
James Lane Allen
James Lane Allen
James Oliver Curwood
James Oppenheim
James Otis
James R. Driscoll
Jane Abbott
Jane Austen
Jane L. Stewart
Janet Aldridge
Jens Peter Jacobsen
Jerome K. Jerome
Jessie Graham Flower
John Buchan
John Burroughs
John Cournos
John F. Kennedy
John Gay
John Glasworthy
John Habberton
John Joy Bell
John Kendrick Bangs
John Milton
John Philip Sousa
John Taintor Foote
Jonas Lauritz Idemil Lie
Jonathan Swift
Joseph A. Altsheler
Joseph Carey
Joseph Conrad
Joseph E. Badger Jr
Joseph Hergesheimer
Joseph Jacobs
Jules Vernes
Julian Hawthrone
Julie A Lippmann
Justin Huntly McCarthy
Kakuzo Okakura
Karle Wilson Baker
Kate Chopin
Kenneth Grahame
Kenneth McGaffey
Kate Langley Bosher
Kate Langley Bosher
Katherine Cecil Thurston
Katherine Stokes
L. A. Abbot
L. T. Meade

L. Frank Baum
Latta Griswold
Laura Dent Crane
Laura Lee Hope
Laurence Housman
Lawrence Beasley
Leo Tolstoy
Leonid Andreyev
Lewis Carroll
Lewis Sperry Chafer
Lilian Bell
Lloyd Osbourne
Louis Hughes
Louis Joseph Vance
Louis Tracy
Louisa May Alcott
Lucy Fitch Perkins
Lucy Maud Montgomery
Luther Benson
Lydia Miller Middleton
Lyndon Orr
M. Corvus
M. H. Adams
Margaret E. Sangster
Margret Howth
Margaret Vandercook
Margaret W. Hungerford
Margret Penrose
Maria Edgeworth
Maria Thompson Daviess
Mariano Azuela
Marion Polk Angellotti
Mark Overton
Mark Twain
Mary Austin
Mary Catherine Crowley
Mary Cole
Mary Hastings Bradley
Mary Roberts Rinehart
Mary Rowlandson
M. Wollstonecraft Shelley
Maud Lindsay
Max Beerbohm
Myra Kelly
Nathaniel Hawthrone
Nicolo Machiavelli
O. F. Walton
Oscar Wilde
Owen Johnson
P.G. Wodehouse
Paul and Mabel Thorne

Paul G. Tomlinson
Paul Severing
Percy Brebner
Percy Keese Fitzhugh
Peter B. Kyne
Plato
Quincy Allen
R. Derby Holmes
R. L. Stevenson
R. S. Ball
Rabindranath Tagore
Rahul Alvares
Ralph Bonehill
Ralph Henry Barbour
Ralph Victor
Ralph Waldo Emmerson
Rene Descartes
Ray Cummings
Rex Beach
Rex E. Beach
Richard Harding Davis
Richard Jefferies
Richard Le Gallienne
Robert Barr
Robert Frost
Robert Gordon Anderson
Robert L. Drake
Robert Lansing
Robert Lynd
Robert Michael Ballantyne
Robert W. Chambers
Rosa Nouchette Carey
Rudyard Kipling
Saint Augustine
Samuel B. Allison
Samuel Hopkins Adams
Sarah Bernhardt
Sarah C. Hallowell
Selma Lagerlof
Sherwood Anderson
Sigmund Freud
Standish O'Grady
Stanley Weyman
Stella Benson
Stella M. Francis
Stephen Crane
Stewart Edward White
Stijn Streuvels
Swami Abhedananda
Swami Parmananda
T. S. Ackland

T. S. Arthur
The Princess Der Ling
Thomas A. Janvier
Thomas A Kempis
Thomas Anderton
Thomas Bailey Aldrich
Thomas Bulfinch
Thomas De Quincey
Thomas Dixon
Thomas H. Huxley
Thomas Hardy
Thomas More
Thornton W. Burgess
U. S. Grant
Upton Sinclair
Valentine Williams
Various Authors
Vaughan Kester
Victor Appleton
Victor G. Durham
Victoria Cross
Virginia Woolf
Wadsworth Camp
Walter Camp
Walter Scott
Washington Irving
Wilbur Lawton
Wilkie Collins
Willa Cather
Willard F. Baker
William Dean Howells
William le Queux
W. Makepeace Thackeray
William W. Walter
William Shakespeare
Winston Churchill
Yei Theodora Ozaki
Yogi Ramacharaka
Young E. Allison
Zane Grey